The
Solution-
Oriented
Woman

The Solution-Oriented Woman

Creating the Life You Want

Pat Hudson
Ph.D.

W · W · Norton & Company · New York · London

First Edition

The text of this book is composed in Galliard with the display set in Windsor Light Condensed and Janson. Composition and manufacturing by the Maple Vail Book Manufacturing Group. Book design by Marjorie J. Flock.

Library of Congress Cataloging-in-Publication Data

Hudson, Patricia O'Hanlon.
    The solution-oriented woman : creating the life you want / Pat Hudson.
      p.   cm.
    Includes bibliographical references and index.
    1. Women—Psychology. 2. Women—Life skills guides. 3. Self-actualization (Psychology) I. Title.
HQ1206.H793   1996
158'.082—dc20   95-33349

ISBN 0-393-03825-4

W. W. Norton & Company, Inc., 500 Fifth Avenue, New York, N.Y. 10110
W. W. Norton & Company Ltd., 10 Coptic Street, London WC1A 1PU

1 2 3 4 5 6 7 8 9 0

To my family:

Lofton
Jessie
Angie
Nick
Zack
Patrick
David

and to my friend, Rhonda

Contents

I.. The Solutions

II.. Putting the Solutions to Work on All Fronts

Acknowledgments

*T*HERE ARE SO MANY PEOPLE to whom I feel grateful for their contributions to this book that it is hard to know where to begin.

Many friends read early versions of the book and discussed the project with me, helping me clarify my concept of what women need: Judith Evnen Benson, Mary Neumann, Gayle Walling Yanney, Paulette Hammerstrom, Cella Quinn, Cathie Siders, Marj Padula-Hall, and Coleen Stice.

There are people who made the book become a reality outside of my office, not only through their professional skills but also through their personal support: my agent, Jim Levine, and my editor, Susan Munro, whose editorial powers were enhanced by Margaret O. Ryan's adept editorial scalpel.

I am especially grateful for my dear friend, Rhonda Applegarth, who has been my business partner and cheered me on when the going got tough; my son-in-law, David Pope, who rescued me from computer problems; my daughter, Angie Hexum, also a writer, who spent hours discussing the ideas with me and kept me on my toes with women's issues; and my father, Lofton Hudson, whose loyal support has been enduring and nurturing since the day I was born.

Thanks also to my sons Zack and Patrick for their support and patience during this project, and my son Nick for the long-distance cheering section he provided.

One

The Problems Women Face

AT 6:30 EVERY MORNING the alarm goes off and the clock radio demands that Suzanne face another busy day. She listens to the news on the radio while preparing herself for the day's work and getting the kids ready for school. She critically examines her face in the mirror. She notices a flaw— there *always* seems to be some flaw—nose not right, puffy eyes, rebellious hair. Undaunted, she assembles her face from various bottles, boxes, and tubes and subjects her hair and ears to the whining whir of the hair dryer. As Suzanne monitors her progress in the mirror, she plans what she will fix for dinner that night. She should insist that Tom make dinner, but they've already had so many arguments about this subject, it seems easier just to do it herself.

As she quietly gets dressed, trying not to wake up her husband—he won't be up for another fifteen minutes—she remembers that she must write a check for lunch money for Jeremy and tonight is soccer for Ashley. She worries that Jeremy's runny nose may make her change her whole schedule to accommodate a doctor's appointment and a day home from school. After she gets the children going on their morning dressing routines, she uses an instant pancake mix to speed up the breakfast process and give herself time to empty the dishwasher and take the chicken breasts out to thaw for dinner. She would have served cereal again, but she was beginning to feel guilty about how often they were eating Captain Crunch. At least Tom will take care of his own breakfast.

Suzanne drops the kids off at school on the way downtown to her office. The kids will stay at the school's day-care facility until Tom picks them up later, and he will also be in charge of chauffeuring the soccer contingent tonight.

By now she has had enough of the day's news from the television and the radio, so she listens to music as she thinks about the business tasks ahead of her: the report she needs to finish for her boss and the collection of regional sales data. Her boss is not a bad fellow. He tries to be fair, but it is clear that he doesn't think of her when a challenging project is available. She will simply have to continue to prove herself and hang in there, until he realizes what a valuable member of the team she is.

As the traffic slows near downtown, the singer on the radio croons, "I'll be yours until the end." She thinks about Tom. *He must care about me, but sometimes I want to give up on him. It's not that he's mean, but I need to be close to him and have a little romance every once in a while to keep me going.* She had thought about divorce from time to time, particularly when she suspected that he was having an affair, but a divorce seemed too drastic and risky. After all, maybe she would never find anyone any better.

Suzanne's mom didn't work until the kids were in school, and for her it was a job, not a career. Like Suzanne, most women today work outside the home. In Suzanne's case, Tom earns more than she does, but for many women the luxury of being secure in a two-paycheck relationship is a thing of the past. A majority of women in the workplace are single, divorced, separated, widowed, or married to men whose annual income is less than $15,000. Even though Suzanne is in charge of the kids, in charge of the house, and the main keeper of the marital relationship, Tom is *there,* and he does many things Suzanne would have to do herself if she were alone.

A Glimpse at Other Books for Women

Helping women like Suzanne has been my mission in life for many years. As a psychologist in practice since 1975, I have been searching for answers to help women. For three years I had a call-in radio show on which the majority of the callers were women. I had already investigated ways to help clients in the office; now I had to come up with answers and solutions at the rate of five shows a week. This was great, because it gave me an excuse to read, read, read. For ideas to help my female callers, I searched in books written for women, I searched in books on feminism, and I searched in books about life and motivation.

The books written for women generally had two flaws. First, they blamed men. Since I, like a majority of women, have, or plan on having, a relationship with one of those creatures that some women's books have labeled as flawed or worse, the answers based on that biased premise were dissatisfying. It really didn't seem all that helpful to decide that things weren't working for her because *he* had a testosterone-induced character blemish.

The second problem with self-help books for women was that they tended to label and blame women as well. Consider the whole concept of *codependency,* which is a worthy concept when describing a spouse who is enabling an alcoholic to continue drinking. However, when any concern for a partner's well-being is labeled codependency, the idea has been taken way too far. Think about the characteristics that are considered codependent: ignoring your own needs for the needs of others; caring about someone else's feelings, successes, and failures; protecting others; taking on too much responsibility. Don't they sound like the qualities that are typical for females in our culture? In her excellent book, *The Mismeasure of Woman,* Carol Tavris points out that the concept of codependency labels typical womanhood as pathological, with the desirable alternative being to act in typical male ways!

When Mary first came to see me, she announced that she was "codependent." A tall, Scandinavian-looking woman in her early forties, she dressed corporate: a suit and sensible pumps. Since she had used the label *codependent,* I expected her to launch into her saga of doormathood—how she had let men walk all over her and covered up their problems by rescuing them. Instead she reported that she had not had a serious relationship in several years and had spent the last two years tending to her dying mother. She had labeled herself as codependent because she was lonely and feeling desperate for a close relationship, particularly since her mother's death.

After talking about the loss of her mother, we focused on ways she could make contact with other human beings. Rather than trying to cure her needs, we found ways for her to meet those needs by meeting more people and participating in relationships of various sorts, such as Big Sisters, sports clubs, and volunteering at a hospital. These activities could provide a wide variety of interpersonal relationships for her and a greater possibility of meeting either a man or a woman to become close to.

When I turned to feminist literature looking for answers, I felt more at home with what I found. I agreed with much of the theorizing about where women's problems came from, but again I felt frustrated. I found myself fussing at the pages. *Okay! Even if you're right about the patriarchal conspiracy, how is this going to help me deal with my family tonight or when someone calls me tomorrow on my show with a problem?* There just didn't seem to be much in the way of solutions, and solutions were what I needed—and what my women callers needed. We didn't need any more clarification about who was to blame or how we had been victims, and throwing off the expectations of our culture seemed more than any one of us was going to be up to in our lifetimes.

The next type of book I investigated dealt with how to find, motivate, or understand yourself in general. I again discovered labels and the implication that we, as people, were victims (mostly of our parents and their dysfunctional families) and they tended to ignore much of the reality of women's experience. Life is different for women than for men. Women are quick to blame themselves. Books that encourage readers to look for what is wrong are not going to help women move away from that self-blaming stance. Even if blame is warranted one place or another, thinking about whose fault something is does not usually give anyone energy for change.

The "Go For It!" books with a business slant appealed to me because they were closer to my ideas about how to create changes, but I also found myself wondering, *Perhaps that might work, but you're not really considering what life is like for women. It can be a bigger challenge for us because the playing field isn't always level.*

There is a joke about the test St. Peter gave people who were lined up to get into heaven. St. Peter said to the first person in line, a man waiting to go through the pearly gates, "You have to pass a little test to get into heaven." The man was upset, but what could he do? So he said, "Okay. Give me the test." St. Peter said, "Spell God." The man said, "That's it? All I have to do is spell God?" "Yes," said St. Peter. The man paused, thinking that this must be some kind of trick, but then cautiously spelled, "*g-o-d.*" "Fine," said St. Peter, "You may enter Heaven." The next person in line, also a man, went through the same procedure, spelled *g-o-d,* and got into heaven.

Then a woman came to the front of the line. When St. Peter told her she would have to take a test, she protested. "You mean to tell me that after I spent my life working twice as hard as any man for half the pay, raising three children by myself after my husband ran off with a younger woman, and taking care of my aging parents until they died, I *still* have to take a test?!" St. Peter said, "Yes, I'm sorry. It's the rules." The woman let out an exasperated breath and said, "Okay. *g-o-d.*" "No," said St. Peter, "Spell *Czechoslovakia.*"

Facts Before Solutions: Women's Realities

When I look at women's lives, it seems to me that what is true for Suzanne is true for many women. She bears primary responsibility for taking care of the everyday needs of her family and marital relationship. She worries about her looks in a way few men do. She is struggling to make herself an invaluable asset to the business for which she works. She questions the value of marriage as a genuine source of support. Suzanne's life is like the one I lived for most of my adult life. It isn't a nightmare and it certainly could be worse. But it could also be better—*a lot better*.

As I searched for answers for my women callers, it became clear to me that the starting point of finding solutions had to be facing the fact that the life experiences women encounter in our culture that are different from what men experience. If the differences between men's and women's realities did not seem important to me, I would have written *The Solution-Oriented Person*. The solutions to *women's* problems must be designed in the context of the social, psychological, and cultural boundaries and barriers that *women* experience.

Like many women, I have had the experience of trying to juggle a career and single parenting. Divorced after sixteen years of marriage, I was a single parent of three children for three years. At the time of the divorce, my daughter was fourteen and my sons were twelve and four years old. (I had another son later and another divorce after ten years in a second marriage.) I remember lying in bed many mornings thinking, *Well, at least I don't have a dog that I have to take out in the snow for a walk.*

Overwhelmed was just one of the many feelings I experienced during those years. *Fearful* about finances, *hopeful* about the future, *relieved* of the struggle that I had felt in the marriage, *guilty* about the unhappiness of my former husband, and *concerned* about the children and what impact the divorce was having on them: All of these feelings crowded my mind.

The Reality of Danger

In addition to all the emotions I was going through, I also felt some concern about my personal safety. Most women in America do not feel safe. I have lived in two houses in the same middle-class neighborhood since the early 1970s. I used to go for walks by myself. Not long ago a woman was raped two blocks from my home. I no longer go for walks alone. The Department of Justice crime statistics report that a forcible rape occurs every five minutes in our country—and most women know their attackers: relatives and friends are responsible for 33 percent of attacks on women in cases where there was a single offender. It is bizarre to refer to people who might be violent toward you as *friend,* but this is another sobering reality of women's lives.

As I dated men after my divorce, the facts about women who have been sexually abused as children would loom in my mind, mostly in terms of safety for my children. Various studies now suggest that 30 to 50 percent of women have experienced sexual abuse as children, and so far the statistics concerning men's childhood sexual abuse are nearing the 20 percent mark. (As more men are willing to talk about these experiences, the numbers may be higher.) A great many of those abused women were in stepfamily situations.

In a quiet moment on a date, as the man was watching a play, a movie, or a ball game, I would find myself observing him intently and thinking, *Would he be the kind of man who could abuse my daughter or my sons? Is he the kind of man who would get drunk and turn into a bully?*

The power of money is often tied to the problems of violence and burden of responsibilities that affect women. I have had friends who felt they could not leave a dangerous marriage because they would be impoverished. The fact that women are still earning only 70 cents for every dollar earned by men is a bitter injustice that keeps many women in painful or even terrifying situations. Thankfully, this inequality is lessening slowly. Nevertheless, what women experience in our culture is still heavily influenced by enforced monetary realities. One of the factors that allowed me to get away from emotionally destructive and unhappy situations was my ability to earn a decent living. Yet, in spite of having a job, one of the things I worried most about, particularly as a single parent, was the uncertainty of self-employment. However, I knew that I could at least support my children and myself. We would always have shelter, food, and clothing—which is a precious advantage and huge relief *not* felt by far too many women.

Challenges in the Workplace

The workplace holds special challenges for women. Besides the smaller paycheck, subtle messages of disrespect are given by the importance of the projects assigned to women, the roles they are asked to play in an organization, or the assumptions made about the priorities women have. A friend of mine was talking to a woman broadcaster on a national television show. The journalist complained that she was often assigned the "lightweight" human interest stories while her male colleagues were assigned stories about international incidents, politics, and economics.

Women's complaints are often dismissed as hormonally motivated—the product of the time of the month rather than a legitimate perception. When women raise issues of concern those above them would rather ignore, they are called "moody."

As you will learn in Chapter 8, more than half of the women in the workplace have reported experiencing sexual harassment, according to *The 9 to 5 Guide to Combating Sexual Harassment*.

A woman from another city came to me for psychotherapy to help her deal with her "low self-esteem." She was an attractive young woman around thirty years old and one of the two woman engineers in a company of men. Several of her colleagues had tried to date her, kiss her, or touch her in some way. One time she had been sitting at a desk looking over plans with a colleague when he suddenly grabbed her and tried to kiss her. She had said in disgust, "Cut it out!" In her view these men were "just a bunch of nerds who finally had some money and didn't know what to do with it. It's kind of pathetic." I wondered how any woman could feel very good about herself in a work environment where she was constantly treated like a brainless sex object.

We discussed several ways in which she could feel better about herself at work: telling people precisely what bothered her (increasing communication skills), making herself do actions outside of work to boost her confidence, such as competing in marathons (increasing self-esteem), lowering her stress through relaxation exercises (reducing stress), and planning potential legal strategies (using the judicial system to stop the harassment). By changing some of her own skills and managing herself physically and emotionally, she held her colleagues responsible for their harassment and she was able to decrease the frequency of their inappropriate responses to her.

The Body Trap

Work realities are different for women, with less pay and sometimes fewer opportunities for developing their talents. And reality is different at home as well. Like Suzanne, women experience the weight of the responsibility for relationships and the care and preservation of the family. Nearly every woman I know does a full day's work and then comes home to do most of the housework and care of the children.

But that is not the only kind of weight women carry. In the all-too-crucial area of physical appearance, women are caught in a bind. If they succeed in looking even somewhat like the unrealistic images that are presented by the media, then they wonder if they are appreciated for anything other than their bodies; if they fail, they feel flawed and unattractive despite their talents and intelligence.

Judy thought that she might have a heart attack in the middle of her step aerobics class. "What am I doing here?" At the age of forty, her body had begun to let her down. She had spent most of her life getting attention from people for her looks, but those kind of responses were definitely declining. She could remember her days of backless halter tops, when men stared at her in restaurants. She wouldn't subject herself to aerobics if she and her husband weren't going on a cruise for their twentieth wedding anniversary. She had heard that people "live in their bathing suits" on cruises. What an awful thought!

As Judy looked in the mirror that spanned the entire wall in front of her, it was impossible not to notice that nearly everyone there was younger than she was. *Look at those outfits! Why would someone want to work out with an elastic strap up her rear end?* Judy was wearing an oversized tee-shirt, stretch pants, and new size 9 cross-trainer shoes. *I can't do this. My feet look like huge, white, gleaming gunboats that are nearly beyond my control. There I go again zagging right when everyone else is zigging left. Oh, great! Pulse time. Well, at least I can dock the gunboats . . . oops, already above the pulse rate I am supposed to be at—my training range. That's no surprise.*

Judy is like so many women who struggle to attain a goal that is even unrealistic for women twenty years younger and nearly impossible for someone her age. As Naomi Wolfe pointed out in *The Beauty Myth,* a generation ago the average model weighed 8 percent less that the average woman. Now she weighs 23 percent less. Advertising, television, movies— and often boyfriends, parents, husbands, friends, and even children—all make their contribution to women's negative feelings about their bodies. The not-so-subtle message that being anything but thin is disgraceful is pervasive. The solutions women create need to include accepting their bodies and keeping them healthy, which does *not* include obsessive dieting.

In my view women are confronted by more challenges than

men. I do not see them as victims, but before effective solutions can be conceived, there has to be an empathic acknowledgment of this fact. In general, women deal with several problems more than men do: violence, sexual harassment, lack of acceptance for their bodies, excessive responsibility for family and relation-ship, and discriminatory pay and practices in work environ-ments. These issues obviously demand political and legal solutions, but that is not where my expertise lies. I help women change their lives—one woman at a time. My hope is that if enough women change their personal circumstances, life for women in our culture will also change for the better.

Designing Your Own Solution-Oriented Approach

As part of improving your life as a woman, you need to identify which areas need help. By asking yourself the following questions, you can decide exactly where to focus the power solutions in your life.

QUESTIONS ABOUT YOUR REALITY

Do I take primary responsibility for the emotional state of my relationship and the well-being of my children?
Do I receive equitable financial treatment in terms of the work I do in my job and at home?
Do I obsess about my physical appearance?
Has violence been a problem for me?
Has my body been violated through abuse?

Whether victimized by a patriarchal culture, our parents, or by our physiology, there *are* solutions. I know about these solutions because for several years I have been doing solution-oriented therapy. This model of therapy focuses on people's strengths and abilities and where they have been *successful* in the past, rather than exploring all their failures in detail. From working with my clients, I have learned that this is the most effective way to solve problems. Solutions don't come from diagnosing difficulties by slapping a label on them and then searching for the culprit who created the difficulties in the first place. After years of working as a solution-oriented therapist and over two decades of helping people (particularly women), I know of many answers that could help Suzanne and other women who have been through so much more. Solutions are what this book is all about.

Solutions fall into four categories: the *thinking* solution, the *acting* solution, the *dreaming* solution, and the *feeling* solution. This book is divided into two parts, first discussing the four solutions and then their applications. The solutions are not steps to be followed in any particular order. Rather, they offer an array of possibilities that you can use in any way you choose to create a cascading effect that sends beneficial ripples of change throughout every area of your personal and work life.

The first ingredient of the solution-oriented approach is the *thinking solution*. We create our own psychological reality by the words we use to describe our experiences and the ideas we have about the nature of reality. Psychological problems do not have a concrete reality in the way the chair I am sitting on does. We *are taught* ideas about what causes us to feel what we feel and do what we do. These ideas change in accordance with whatever psychological theory is popular at the time. For example, in the Freudian heyday, people's problems originated from what happened to them in early childhood. The way to solve a problem was to just let the client talk (free associate). This process, psychoanalysis, often took years and was very expensive. We are still dealing with the assumptions that problems are *caused by* a person's childhood. Other therapies (rational emotive therapy, cognitive therapy) focused on the irrationality of the client's thinking process as the cause of problems. Meanwhile behavior therapists saw problems and their resolutions as determined by the number of times some action was rewarded, ignored, or punished. Nowadays, the most popular new forms of therapy are brief and narrative therapies—including my specialty, solution-oriented therapy. Solution-oriented therapists tend to bypass the underlying cause of a problem. Instead, the therapist might guide the client to look for times when the situation was better or encourage the client to experiment with what might change the difficulty.

What you believe based upon the prevailing psychological theory can either prevent or promote change. Ideas regarding causes create a reality for you. Exploring and changing the questions you ask yourself and the theories you create in response to your experiences can change your life in a surprisingly powerful way.

The *action solution* focuses on using action words to communicate more clearly. We often communicate in vague and abstract ways. For example, if you say to your partner, "I want more support from you," but don't say how "support" translates into concrete actions, your partner is left to his own ideas. He may try various actions that he thinks of as being supportive, but never stumble upon the actions *you* consider supportive. In using the action solution, you translate vague complaints and requests into "videotalk." I use the image of videotalk to emphasize communications about actions—what you could see or hear on a videotape. Using our "support" example, what could you see and hear if you saw a videotape of someone being supportive?

Using an action solution also involves changing some of your *patterns of actions*. Patterns are behaviors you do over and over again in relationships. If your actions are not getting the results you want, notice what action patterns you do and change your part of the pattern. For example, if you find that repeatedly you are accused of being "bossy" in a romantic relationship, then you might notice what behaviors you and your partner are doing that keep that pattern going. You might notice that you give directions when the two of you are in the car; you might notice that your partner refuses to make decisions about purchases for your home so that you find yourself making those decisions; or you might find that you are making many suggestions about his health and his business decisions.

Patterns are different from simple actions in that you do them *with* someone else and either you or that other person has a part to play in continuing the pattern. In the bossy example, you could practice not offering guidance or he might practice telling you what he intended to do as soon as a subject came up. Even if your partner does not get any help for this problem, you might be able to change the pattern by changing your part. If you refuse to tell him what to do, he might just start to figure that out on his own. The goal of the acting solutions is to discover what results you can achieve by changing your actions.

The third solution is the *dreaming solution,* and it can be used simultaneously with the first two solution categories. By getting to know your own unconscious mind through creative daydreaming, paying attention to your night dreams, and practicing self-hypnosis, you can learn how to elicit this realm that is normally not available to you. Then you can have *all* parts of your inner self moving towards solutions.

By using the first three methods of the solution-oriented woman, you can typically solve most of your problems. Following a painful time in your life, however, you may still feel grief or sadness about what has happened to you. It's during such a time that you need to use the *feeling solution,* which includes acknowledging your feelings and creating rituals to bring healing and comfort.

The rest of the book (Part II) demonstrates how to apply these solution categories to typical problems women face. These problem areas are not intended to represent a comprehensive coverage of women's concerns but a selection based on those issues that radio-show callers and clients in counseling mention most often.

Once you understand how to apply these solution methods to your life, you will be able to solve most of the difficulties that you, as a woman, face. I want to give you more than formula answers to particular problems. I want to give you flexible tools to apply to any relationship problem, any personal, psychological, or work challenge that confronts you in the course of your life as a woman. What I ask from you is the willingness to experiment. I know that if you use these ideas, you can create the life you want and deserve.

..1

The Solutions

Two

The Thinking Solution

*A*NNE WAS GOING THROUGH pre-divorce hell. For a year she had been so depressed that every time she would start to eat her throat clogged and closed the way it does when you're about to cry. She had lost thirty pounds and cried her way through a three-month period. She believed her misery was caused by her failed marriage. She had spent the summer separated from her husband, Grant, but they were trying to reconcile in September.

She had tried to "figure out" the marriage, understand Grant and herself, and look for the underlying motives in what was happening between them. She kept thinking, *There must be something wrong with me that I can't be happy with this man.* She scolded herself for not tolerating the lack of intimacy between them or rising above the corrosive quality of her husband's frequent criticism. She wondered if she were too sensitive, she wondered why she couldn't just buckle down and accept the situation. She thought to herself over and over again, *If I could just understand why he is the way he is and why I am the way I am, some fog might blow away, revealing the love I yearn for.*

For two years they had gone to therapy—in fact, they had tried three different therapists with three different approaches to solving problems. Like so many women, Anne had taken responsibility for trying to save the marriage by initiating the therapy process. With their first therapist they had talked about the families they grew up in and they tried to have fights for the therapist, who wanted to see firsthand how they handled conflict. These "on demand" fights were difficult to generate because they didn't feel close enough to lather up real hostility. With the second therapist, Anne and Grant were asked to bring in their parents. His parents would not be into "any such non-sense" so only Anne's parents came. Anne and Grant talked about patterns that had occurred in their parents' marriages and even their grandparents' marriages, because the therapist believed that these patterns were passed on like genes. Anne tried to see how she was expressing her parents' conflicts, but it just didn't ring the bell. She *wasn't* reenacting her parents' marriage, so it was hard to get help with their problem since it didn't fit the therapist's usual solution. The third therapist at least stopped talking about the couple's childhoods and their parents, since that had not been effective for the last two rounds of therapy. Instead they tried to make some headway in what was going on right then and there.

Grant had difficulty adjusting to therapy. His inability to respond made him look a little worse in Anne's eyes, particularly since she was so responsive to therapy. But they still spent eight months giving the therapy one last sincere shot. It was excruciatingly frustrating to Anne that, with all the understanding they had gained in therapy as to the "why" of their problems, no improvement had occurred in the marriage. Finally the marriage died its own death and they divorced.

Anne experienced the divorce as a relief from the futile struggle of trying to create change by understanding the innermost tickings of herself and her spouse. I met Anne three years later and introduced her to the solution-oriented approach. She told me that if she had had another alternative to the kinds of therapy they were getting, they might have been able to save their marriage.

The Futile Search for the Whys and the Wherefores

Like Anne, I use to be very interested in the why of problems. As the child of a traditional pastoral counselor (a brilliant one at that—my father wrote twenty-two books on religion and mental health), I spent my childhood hearing clever speculations on people's underlying motives.

When I was thirteen, my father went to a workshop on hypnosis. He had volunteered to be a demonstration subject. He was about to turn fifty, had some arthritis in his knees, and wanted the hypnotherapist to help him understand its origin— thereby ridding him of the arthritis. Over the dinner table Dad reported a real breakthrough.

"As I sat there on the stage, I began to cry. I kept seeing my mother in the nursing home. I remembered her trying to keep me there whenever I visited; I could literally hear the sounds of her yelling for me as I walked down the wooden stairs. When I came out of the trance my legs didn't hurt anymore, and for the first time I felt free of all the sadness and conflict I had felt about my mother and her anger towards me for putting her in a nursing home."

Dad's eyes were glistening with excitement and he did seem somehow changed. I was impressed. Of course, this was only one of hundreds of stories that I heard around the dinner table at home and in restaurants when we would go out with other therapists. My teen-age conclusion was: the way to solve problems was to uncover the pivotal event that had left the person so screwed up in the first place. Thereafter I committed many years of my life to searching for causes.

By September of 1981 I had already spent nine years helping people excavate their pasts in search of that pivotal event. It seemed to me that people could get better other ways, but the pivotal-event approach was supposed to be the "royal road." I had the attitude that anything less was just a so-so way to change. However, I couldn't help but notice that searching for causes was not doing me a bit of good in the marital crisis I was personally facing! That month I attended my first solution-oriented therapy workshop based on the work of the psychiatrist Milton Erickson.

Truth IS Relative

Now *this* was something new. In the solution-oriented perspective that grew from Erikson's work, people were not viewed as being sick at the core, warped by their history, but as having strengths and abilities; the clients, not the therapists, had the answers within them and were their own experts; and there was not one true insight that would encompass all that the client needed to know. Shocking! As the workshop continued, the new ideas I was hearing bumped into the old ideas I'd taken for granted for decades. I had spent my life looking for the Holy Grail of *the* true insight. I had considered insight as palpable and concrete as a silver chalice. I had believed that ideal love existed and that I could learn how to understand and accept my partner unconditionally. Meanwhile, the workshop leader was saying that there was no Holy Grail, no absolute truth.

There and then I discovered the one insight that *has* changed my life and my response to nearly every human interaction since: in psychology there is no single "truth"; psychological reality is made up! Each person has his or her current view of the truth, the whole field of psychotherapy has its own favorite view of the truth, and these change with whatever is in vogue in popular culture or in psychotherapy at the time. Our labels of ourselves as narcissistic, obsessive-compulsive, depressive, or even codependent are made-up ideas. There is no truth, no cause, no label that you have to find to make your life work right *now*. This was a dizzying relief for me and a huge disappointment. The lack of an answer became in itself a new answer for me—my own Holy Grail. It might be thought of as the Zen of psychotherapy. Had I just wasted the last nine years of my life doing "insight" therapy? Should I send all my clients a recall notice telling them that I was wrong, the answers that we had come to in therapy were all made up?

I decided against the recall notice, but I did apply the new ideas to my own life. Once I understood that I would really never know why my husband (or anyone else) was doing what he was doing *and that I didn't have to know,* I felt deep relief. In the past I would upset myself by thinking, *Why is he doing whatever he is doing—doesn't he love me?* Usually the "truth" piped up in my mind, *No, he is damaged and he can't love you—* and then I would get *really* upset. I was still very disappointed in our relationship, but at least I no longer had to spend my every waking moment trying to figure out why.

This shift in thinking did not save that marriage, but it was the beginning of a new era for me as a person and as a therapist. It also contained the basis of the thinking solution I want to give to you.

For starters, give up your explanations or at least hold onto them with a very relaxed grip. You are never going to find one single and absolute truth. If you bumped your head on an open cupboard door while cooking, you would discover the hard reality of the door—it is solid. Except for the most far-out philosophy major, we would all agree that the door is reality— the truth. But what about the explanations you find to explain why you knocked into the cupboard door? Because you are neurologically challenged? Because you have a self-defeating personality? Because you wanted someone's attention? Because you were anxious and preoccupied? There are a lot of explana- tions you could generate. One is potentially as real or true as the others. It may be that all might have some accuracy. I would probably explain my own bumping into a cupboard door as my clumsiness (although I prefer the term "neurologically chal- lenged"). Yet I do have many things that occupy my mind, and I do wish my mother were still around to kiss my "owey." How could I say with certainty which explanation was the most powerful and accurate at that moment?

Why do you generally act the way you do? Is it because of how you were raised? Is it because of your hormones? Is it because something in your partner reminds you of something in your parent? Is it because you need to get in touch with your inner child? Is it because our patriarchal society judges you according to a male standard? Give it up! If I had a snarled ball of strings, it would be hard to tell which string was the longest. Psychological explanations are like a snarl of strings. It is very difficult to tell which is the most important, most accurate explanation. *You will never know whether your explanation is the most accurate. And until you let go of the futile and exhausting search for psychological truth, you cannot truly claim your life for change.* If it seems too hard to relinquish your ideas about why people do what they do, maybe just loosening your grip on those ideas will help. Keep an open mind. Letting go of the search for certainty has felt very freeing to me, and I hope you will feel that too.

Since psychological reality is highly relative—made up of each person's current beliefs—the goal of this solution-oriented approach is to either avoid explanations or show you how to *make up* explanations in a way that will let you find solutions, let you create the life you want, let you be free of having to find the truth before you can move on to anything else.

Giving Up Blame for Accountability

One of the barriers to change is blame. If you tend to look for the culprit in each and every conflict, then that kind of thinking may be part of what you need to change. This doesn't mean you shouldn't hold others accountable for their behavior, but neither men nor women respond well to blame: women tend to take on the blame and berate themselves; men tend to withdraw and become defensive. (I realize that I just put forth one of those theories that I told you to give up, but bear with me.) When someone has offended or hurt you, the alternative to blame is to hold the person accountable, which means making a request about a change in behavior you expect and requiring the person to rectify the situation or to make amends. This shift in thinking gets you out of the "fault swamp" and leads to something to do. If necessary, you may need to add consequences, assuming the person's behavior continues to be offensive, hurtful, or abusive.

Matt has been laid off of his job for two weeks. When Betsy comes home from work, she discovers Matt sitting on the couch watching television, like he has been doing every day since he stopped working. It is clear that he has not chosen to shave again. Betsy thinks, *If he applied for a job today looking like that, he would not have gotten it, unless the job was at a place that specializes in undercover investigations.*

How might Betsy respond to this situation? She could blame Matt for not having applied for a job; she could blame his family for not having instilled hope in their boy; she could blame herself for letting him get away with turning into a depressed couch potato. *Or* Betsy could hold Matt accountable for doing a job search each day.

Going for the last option, Betsy asks, "Did you apply for a job today?" Matt shakes his head no and keeps his eyes on the television.

Betsy walks over to the television set and firmly pushes the power button. "I was watching that!" Matt protests, but he can see that Betsy is not going to be put off this time.

"Matt, I don't insist that you find a job, but sitting on the couch all day is not good for either of us. I ask that you do something to get a job at least once each day. You can call an employment service, you can look in the paper and follow up on leads there, or you can contact an old boss. But, no matter what you are going to do the rest of the day, I really must insist that you make one good faith effort by noon each day."

Matt sighs. "I know you're right, honey, but I've been listening to the news everyday about unemployment here in California. There is nothing out there, so I stay home." (Matt is blaming the economy.)

Betsy feels bad for Matt in his discouragement, but she is determined not to let him grow roots into that couch. "Are you willing to go out by noon everyday and look for a job?" Betsy does not want to put herself in the position of mothering Matt, but at the same time she is unwilling to let things go on this way. She avoids blaming, but tries to hold Matt accountable.

"If I go out everyday by noon and make one application, will you spare me the lecture about looking for a job when you get home?"

Although Betsy feels that his characterizations of their discussions as "lectures" is unjust, she agrees to this condition, since her goal is to get a commitment from Matt to look for a job. And when Betsy holds Matt accountable for looking for a job, he is more likely to find a job. But, most importantly, their relationship is not ruined in the process.

The Explanation Trap

Think about the last time you had a disagreement with your partner. Imagine how many different reasons you could attribute the fight to: you could have decided that the person was trying to control you or take advantage of you; you could have concluded that he or she was being selfish—not considering your feelings; you could have thought that the person was unable to act any other way due to childhood experiences; or you could have assumed that the person was just plain mean. Like the snarled strings, many of these explanations might fit for the conflict, but it would be hard to know which was the very best explanation.

The difficulties with fights about explanations is that you can get into dueling explanations. Both ideas seem plausible and, particularly to someone not having the argument, reasonable.

Donald is heading home on a Friday night in rush-hour traffic. *At last the weekend,* he thinks, as he pulls into the drive-way of his suburban, mortgaged, two-story home. Donald works in sales and his wife, Christie, is a cog in the massive corporate machinery. Donald opens a beer as soon as he comes in the door. Christie is already home, dinner well underway, sipping her Friday night glass of wine. She follows Donald into the bedroom to talk to him while he changes into his jeans.

"Donald, I think we should talk about how we're going to spend this weekend. The last two weekends we haven't gotten the basic chores done, and I'm concerned that I will start an-other week on Monday feeling overwhelmed because so much needs to be done. The lawn needs mowing, the carpets haven't been vacuumed in two weeks, and I could write a grocery list in the dust on the dining room table."

"You'd better not. It would be hard to take the table to the market," Donald quips from the closet door where he is hang-ing his tie on the rack.

"Don't do that, Donald. Every time we start to have a discus-sion about the household duties, you either joke your way out of it or say you'll do it and then don't!"

"Look, I have told you that I value my time off and that I don't want my weekends spent trying to fulfill some Blooming-dale's dream you have about how our house should look!"

"That's just not fair! I worked all week too! We should be splitting these duties 50–50!"

This might sound all too familiar to you. Later I will talk about how to find a solution to this conflict, but first let's look at all the ways Christie might search for the unattainable truth that would explain her husband's behavior in this scene.

From a behavioral point of view, the problem could be de-fined in terms of "reinforcement"—Donald's relief at not doing the housework is more reinforcing for him than the "punish-ment" he receives from Christie's distress. Christie, meanwhile, is receiving reinforcement from arguing with Donald, because at least he really participates in a heated discussion. In fighting, she feels connected with him, even if, in the end, he doesn't do any more household tasks than before.

From the point of view that our childhoods cause our adult lives, it could be that Christie is trying to undo the injustices she saw perpetrated upon her mother in her childhood home. She noticed her mother doing "all the work" while her father played golf and said that, after all, he was making more money so that her mother should bear the burden of the house.

A feminist explanation would say that Donald's behavior is a product of the fact that he came from a sexist family and thinks housework is the domain of women; furthermore, Christie is also influenced by the sexist images that a woman is not a good woman unless her home is clean.

The men's movement would explain that, because his own father was usually absent from home, Donald had no model of participatory partnership. Also, since a man must break from his attachment to his mother, Donald could be seen as living out his need to grasp his manhood by refusing to do what Christie wished.

From a psychodynamic perspective, Donald might be rebelling unconsciously against what he perceived to be his mother's controlling and critical attitude toward him when he was growing up.

From a transactional analysis point of view, Christie's "parent" is uselessly talking to Donald's "child" and they both need to move to adult-to-adult communications.

Whew! Searching for why Donald did not want to do housework on the weekend could drive you nuts! You may notice that none of those explanations supplies an obvious solution.

Like Christie, you too cannot know why; even if you did, it would probably not do you one bit of good. I spent a decade as a psychotherapist helping people understand the reasons for their feelings and behavior by giving insight into their past. Based on all those thousands of hours working with clients in this way, I can report that *understanding* rarely produces change. This is particularly true if you are hoping to make something change in less than six months, and in the age of managed care, if it takes six months or more, you'll probably be paying for it yourself.

As I let go of the explanations for what was wrong with my clients and focused more on their strengths and abilities, my methods became increasingly brief. The journey to solutions did not have to be a long trip after all. When clients came to my office, it seemed as though they were looking for directions. Say you are lost in New York City at 57th and Lexington Avenue, and you want help finding the quickest way to get to your destination, which is Lincoln Center. After searching for a friendly face in the crowd, you might ask for help from a person who turns out to be a traditional therapist. "I'm trying to find Lincoln Center," you tell her. "Can you tell me how to get there?" The therapist responds with a question, "Where did you come from?" "Washington, D.C.," you obligingly answer, "but how do I get to Lincoln Center?" The therapist asks another question, "Is your family from there and did they like D.C.?" "Yes, they are, and yes, they do," you continue, "but *how do I get to Lincoln Center?*" Now concerned about the rising tension in your voice, the therapist asks, "How do you feel about being lost?"

Solution-oriented therapists help you find your way to the Lincoln Centers of life—if that is where you want to go—rather than focusing on what made you this way. To become a solution-oriented woman, you will learn to give up dwelling on the past, look at where you want to go, and find the quickest ways to get there. I do not want to imply that it might not be interesting and fun to look at what made you the way you are, but when you are interested in change, then you probably want to change the quickest way possible. The changes you might want can be in the external area of actions and interactions or in the internal areas of the unconscious and feelings. Being solution-oriented can touch all those areas.

When people in my practice started to change quickly, I became concerned that perhaps the changes would not last or that the clients would feel less satisfied with the therapy. To find out what happened to my clients, I conducted follow-up customer satisfaction surveys. I found that the changes remained intact and that the clients were happy with the results of the brief therapy even a year later.

It isn't easy to stop yourself from making up your own psychological theories about the whys and wherefores of your experience. Our culture has taught us well—perhaps too well—how to do that. What's worse, as women we reflexively ask, "What's wrong with *me?*" as Anne did in her marriage. Thinking solutions start with a growing awareness of these thinking pitfalls. It is human nature to generate these explanatory kinds of ideas, so don't scold yourself for not being "theory-free." You can, however, take a step back from those theories, recognizing that there are many ways to explain things, and start to make up new theories that are not so negative.

For example, how could Christie and Donald make up theories about each other in the least destructive way? Christie could look for an explanation that would not label Donald as a selfish jerk who doesn't care about the house. She could view Donald's weekend behavior as protecting their relationship from the deadening effects of routine and chores. She could agree that Donald did need the time to recuperate from work and join him in some of the fun. I'm not saying that she should do all the housework, only that she might find ways of viewing Donald's behavior that would leave her less irritated. She could still ask for productive actions and, at the same time, explore with him other ways to make home life fun.

From Donald's perspective, Christie's values had seemed shallow and difficult to attain given their dual career life together. His shift in perspective might be that, in marriage, you may be happier looking for compromises when you have different values. He might decide Christie's commitment to a clean house is her way of doing a "good marriage," not controlling him and insisting her values rule their weekends. Donald's alternative to convincing Christie that her values are wrong could be to explore the minimal chores he would have to do to help Christie feel less overwhelmed.

There are nearly always alternative psychological ideas to explain why people do what they do, so make up ones that lead to change or at least make you feel less distress.

Christie and Donald were eventually able to come to a compromise. Donald would do things around the house until 3:00 p.m. on Saturday and then Christie would not ask him to participate in any other chore activities until 3:00 p.m. on Sunday. That way, Donald would know that he could have twenty-four hours to himself and Christie would know that she wasn't being abandoned to do all the chores herself.

Naming Is Creating

The first problem with psychological theories is that you can waste a great deal of energy and yet never know the truth. The second problem is that just naming something as "the truth" creates it. *Naming* shapes your ideas and creates something that exists in psychological reality—not physical reality, but psychological reality.

Over the years I have noticed that people who have some vague unhappiness become much more upset when they see a television show about the problem. For example, I might have a client who feels somewhat unfulfilled and unfocused. She then sees a television show on depression. After the show the client begins to notice that she *does not* sleep as well as she used to, she *does* feel lonely, and she *does* feel like her life is useless. Before the television show the woman needed to work on her marriage and on changing her career to something more fulfilling. Labeling herself as depressed, she now feels that she has a serious, perhaps medical, problem. Naming her feelings "depression" creates a more severe view of her difficulties than is warranted.

Another example: fifteen years ago I had never had a client

with a "codependency" problem. Five years ago that was the main complaint that brought women to my office.

Margaret was in her fifties. She was happy with her life. She had devoted herself to her children, all three of whom were grown, and to her husband. Her kids had all graduated from college and two were married. They had turned out well enough for her to feel she had done a good job being their mother.

She was baking a pie when daughter Karen called. "Mom, I've been attending a class on codependency. I feel very concerned for you. You have spent your whole life living for other people. Your main concerns in life are *other people's* concerns. How can you possibly be happy? I think you need counseling. Dad has used you to take care of everything for him—his laundry, the bills, cooking, and housework. Meanwhile he has been impatient rather than appreciative and controlled you by controlling all the money. You've given up your whole life!"

Margaret was stunned. "Karen, I'm *not* unhappy. I *like* my life."

The conversation ended at an impasse, with Karen trying to convince her mother that she could not really be that happy and Margaret defending herself. But Margaret continued to think about what Karen had said and found herself feeling more and more dissatisfied. Once the beast had been named, it followed her from room to room, cornering her when she was idle.

I am not suggesting that you avoid learning new ideas or that new concepts might not be useful. I am saying that you should realize that by naming or labeling something you create a reality that may become self-fulfilling and make you less happy, not happier.

When I was in family therapy for my marriage of sixteen years, the therapist was convinced that I wanted out of my marriage because my parents had never really been happy and I was fulfilling their unacknowledged desires by undoing my own marriage. Although my parents were not deliriously happy, they seemed definitely above average. They kidded each other a lot and had many common interests: books, plays, travel. They clearly seemed happier with their marriage than I was with mine! But the theory that the therapist presented about my parents' marriage preyed on my mind for a while. I kept looking for evidence that his theory was right. Surely there must be some underlying discontent in my parents' marriage that I was fulfilling by wanting to divorce my husband. After searching for some hidden discontent in my parents, I finally "went to bat" for the fact that I no longer wanted to live with my husband. However, naming the problem as my parents' hidden problem slowed me down for some months in a futile search.

Once something has been named, we automatically look for evidence of it and, with any luck at all, we find it. If someone said to you, "Your husband is a weak man," don't you think you might start noticing behaviors that could be labeled as weak? It is much like the medical student phenomenon. As the student doctor reads the text about a disease, she begins to think, "Gee! I have a lot of those symptoms, too!" (I try to avoid articles that list the symptoms of rare, hard-to-diagnose diseases for just this reason.) Einstein said that believing is seeing. If you believe in a particular psychological concept, you will be able to gather evidence for it—and that includes this one!

Barb and Steve had taken their son Josh to a psychologist, because Josh was not making friends in school and did not seem happy. After one family session and one session alone with Josh, the therapist concluded that "the two of you don't want to be married." Prior to this session they did have some things to work on in their marriage, but after the psychologist's pronouncement, they had a lot more to work on! I wondered if the psychologist had just come from a family therapy workshop centering on children's problems being the result of their parents' marital difficulties. It took four sessions with me to put this comment behind them, because they had begun to question satisfactions that they had together. Maybe-I-don't-really-enjoy-my-spouse-like-I-think-I-do thoughts crept into their minds. Fortunately, they were able get on with enjoying life together again.

This kind of situation is why many people are wisely suspicious of "shrinks," therapists, and counselors. It is possible that trying to make things better will make them worse, particularly if a therapist likes to make pronouncements about issues that you did not come to therapy to discuss in the first place! Naming something as a psychological disease will either create the disease or at least turn you into an investigator who is fearfully on the lookout for evidence that confirms what you were told. It's similar to when a doctor says, "With a hemoglobin count like yours, you must be tired all the time." If you were not tired before you heard that comment, chances are high that you will notice some fatigue soon after it!

Be cautious and leery of experts—even me! Trust your own judgment, do your own investigating, and know that, even if someone with "doctor" in front of his or her name says something is true, it isn't necessarily so. I don't mean that you should doubt your doctor if she tells you she saw a tumor on your X-ray, but if someone tells you that you have a tendency to be depressed, I'd be careful not to believe that too easily.

In examining your thinking about a particular problem, you might find it illuminating to look at the assumptions contained in how you describe it and the questions you ask yourself.

Trading In Used Questions for New Questions

Stacey was depressed. As she was lying in her bed one night, she thought about Bob. They had lived together for a year and then he had moved out. He said that he couldn't stand her smothering attention and her jealousy. As she listened to the traffic outside her apartment, and the muted sounds of a neighbor watching television, she kept asking herself over and over again: "What's wrong with me? Things seemed so perfect at first—we had so much in common. Why did I screw this up? Why am I such a loser with men?"

Look at Stacey's questions. The assumption underlying her questions is that *she* ruined the relationship and that this failure was not confined to her relationship with Bob, but a trend. She believes, at this point in her thinking, that she is permanently flawed when it comes to relationships with men. The effect of her "why" questions is to depress her further, create more hopelessness, solidify the blame she takes for what went wrong.

If Stacey has to lie in bed feeling like a bundle of garbage the trash man wouldn't even take, what would be better questions she might ask herself? Let's look at "what" and "how" questions and see where they lead.

The edges of light from passing cars peek around the blinds, as Stacey thinks, *How do I keep myself feeling like such a lump? It's been a month since Bob left and I still haven't called a single friend. I used to have such a satisfying routine, walking daily with a friend, eating healthy food, going out on the weekends. Maybe what I should do is go back to those things that made me feel good before I met Bob. Lying here for the last month trying to figure out what went wrong hasn't gotten me anywhere but down! Tomorrow I'm going to call Marlene and see if she wants to walk, and I'm going to stop at the store and get some veggies and fruit. Maybe after dinner I'll see if Geri wants to go out next weekend.*

"How" questions lead to things to *do*. Thinking that leads to actions is thinking that will lead to solutions. "What" questions can also lead to positive change, as Stacey discovers when she follows her "how" questions with these.

Closing her eyes, Stacey pictures Bob's irritated face. *What made Bob so irritated? What kind of patterns did we get into that made things between us so difficult? If he came home fifteen minutes later than usual, I would say—in a tone that was, I have to admit, accusing—"Where have you been?" I knew that he had had a relationship with a woman in his office and I was always afraid he would go back to her. I wonder what would have happened if I had talked about my fears rather than accusing him of keeping her as a back-up girlfriend. It's too late to salvage the relationship with Bob, but the next time I fall in love, I'm going to talk about my fears openly rather than harping and accusing repeatedly. And what kind of things did Bob do that made me more insecure? Perhaps I could have asked him not to talk about his relationship with the woman at work or to agree not to talk to her about anything other than business. Even though I am sad about losing Bob, I realize now that I could have changed my behavior with him, and I think I could make a difference in a new relationship if I started to get into this kind of mess again.*

The "what" and "how" questions lead to ways to make a difference. Notice the basic difference in the assumptions that underlie these three types of questions. Asking *why* assumes that what you are asking about exists in the first place: "Why do I have a depression?" There is an assumption that some psychological state exists independent of actions—you "have" versus "do" depression. Asking *what* and *how* questions in a psychological context assumes that, although you might identify a feeling state—such as when you are in a better mood—there are actions that create your feelings: "*What* do I usually do to feel better?" "*How* can I change my mood today?" Asking why might lead to understanding, but what and how lead to actions that create change.

The feelings we focus on and the questions we ask about those feelings tend to expand them. Whether positive or negative, whatever we focus upon increases.

After my husband of ten years moved out with little warning, I found myself getting worked up about things I hadn't even noticed before. Instead of dwelling on the betrayal I felt or his unwillingness to seek therapy, I became incensed over the things he had failed to do over the years: never snow-blowing the driveway for me so I could go to work; only going with me twice to the hospital when my mother was in intensive care for a month; rarely working on home repairs or taking the cars in for service. Every time I handled something on my own, I would get worked up thinking how this was no different from when I had been married to him—and then I would get angry all over again. I had to make a concerted effort not to dwell on how little I had held him accountable for adult partnership in our marriage, because every time I thought about it, I would get upset. Very unproductive! I decided that every time I thought of these issues, I would ask myself, *What have you learned about the way you act in relationships and how could you avoid these difficulties in the future?* This kept me focused on my power to make a difference in the future rather dissipating my energy in futile ruminations over past injustices. Rather quickly my anger about these peripheral problems subsided. Then I was able to deal with the more cogent legal and financial concerns I needed to be angry about. I learned through my own experiences that whatever I focused on *expanded,* so I chose to point my focus carefully.

The more I worked on projects during that period of my life, the more productive I was. If I threw myself into writing or changing some aspect of my business, I would get renewed energy for doing more and my sense of mastery and success would expand. This doesn't mean that I ignored my grief, but I did not particularly *work* at grieving. For most people, grief happens when it happens. You don't have to knock yourself out to get to grieve.

If you feel stuck with a particular problem but want to get on with your life, change what you focus on. If you want to get over an upset or a loss or make progress towards a goal, keep in mind that what you pay attention to will grow. If you want to be a good student, focus on studying and, sure enough, your performance will improve. If you want a relationship, focus on noticing potential partners and, sure enough, the likelihood of getting a partner will increase. If you think about "how" and "what" questions, you generate action answers that can change your life. If what you are thinking isn't helping you, deliberately move your thinking in another direction by the questions that you allow yourself to ponder.

Mythmaking

How you explain feelings and actions to yourself has meaning in your life. Why not create explanations that will help you change or manage a transition more effectively? I think of this as "mythologizing" your life. Joseph Campbell wrote about creating a myth of your life when he discussed what constitutes the hero's journey. Rethink the explanation, the myth, you believe about an episode in your life so that you can create a story around it that converts a disappointment into a victory. As Campbell points out, the hero goes on a journey that involves a series of ordeals, ultimately returning to his homeland with some object or learning of great value.

When a therapist friend of mine, Brenda, faced the embarrassment and sense of failure of a second divorce, we talked about what she might bring back from that ordeal to create a feeling of heroism for herself. There were a few things she thought she might bring back: as a therapist, she would now, with firsthand knowledge of mid-life crisis, be better able to help others dealing with the same issue. Another valuable outcome would be the ability to *avoid* creating attitudes and stories about *all* men based upon bad experiences with her particular husband. A third way Brenda mythologized her experience was to view the divorce as a release from a relationship that did not support her growth. Brenda was too committed to the relationship to ever consider ending it "just" for her own growth, but she was able to recognize the important personal benefit once her husband had ended it.

Fourth, Brenda examined where her romantic ideas came

from to see if there was some wisdom she could gain from rethinking these ideals. She concluded that she could finally relinquish her mother's obsession with love and romance. Those ideals had motivated her to choose romance over practical considerations of what was good for her as a person or as a woman wanting to succeed in her marriage *and* her career. Now she freed herself of this burden, no longer needing to work so hard to keep that romance going. Brenda began to sense what might be possible for her to accomplish as she expanded her love beyond the narrow confines of a single relationship to groups—clients, students, and friends. Her myth—explanation or story of her divorce—was that she was now finally free to experience more of her abilities and talents than she had ever before in her life. This did not mean that Brenda would not have another relationship; it meant that she could put romance aside, at least for a while, to make a bigger contribution to the world (and herself) that did not include romantic happiness.

This helped Brenda stay out of the swamp she feared she would sink into; it has acted like a flashlight in the dark, guiding her to terrain that helped her feel stronger rather than weaker. By looking for the positive mythology you can create about many of your challenging situations, as Brenda was doing, you can expand the positive things you focus on—*and* experience.

SOLUTION-ORIENTED THINKING
Principles and Pathways

Popular beliefs change ▪ Begin to recognize how something you believed was true five or ten years ago is no longer true—which means there is no single truth.

Can you identify the ideas you had when you were a teenager about an issue, such as men-women relationships, that are different today? How have those ideas changed at different stages in you life?

Accountability is more effective than blame ▪ Avoid blame; instead hold people accountable.

What is a blaming label that you have had for yourself or someone in a relationships (passive-aggressive, sexist, selfish, jealous, etc.)? Could you think of ways to translate that label into actions and then hold yourself or someone else accountable by your creating consequences for changing those actions?

Many ideas can explain psychological events ▪ Think up as many explanations as possible to attribute to one episode of conflict. Notice how they each lead to a different understanding while producing no change.

Consider an action in a personal or work relationship that bothers you. What are three different explanations you could create for why that person did what he did?

Naming is creating ▪ Since whatever you pay attention to *expands,* focus on thoughts and activities that will help you feel better and accomplish your goals.

What are some of the labels you have had for yourself? Can you think of any way in which you might have done more actions that fit that label once you decided you were that way?

Questions block or promote change ▪ Change your "why" questions to "what" and "how" questions so that they point towards solutions. Consider anything that is not going well for you in your life. Notice any explanations ("whys") you may have for that event or series of events. Apply "what" and "how" questions.

What are you doing when this is less of a problem? How could you change your actions so that this is no longer a problem for you?

We create myths about our histories and our futures ▪ Create explanations that will lead to positive actions and feelings.

What is an explanation that you have about some disappointment in your life? Is there any way you could change that explanation (myth) so that you might realize that in some way you are or can be a hero because of that event?

Three

The Action Solution

G ERALD WAS HOPING that this evening would please Christina. For the last few months she had been saying that she wanted more romance. The atmosphere of the restaurant seemed like just the thing for her. Dim lighting—so dim, in fact, he wondered if it would ruin the moment if he put the candle between his glasses and the menu so he could read the exorbitant prices. Aromas of garlic, butter, and wine filled the air, the bottle of red wine breathed, or, at that price, sighed longingly next to them. Surely Christina would be happy. The waiter commented, "Good choice," after they each ordered. Gerald had been waiting for this moment to give his wife a locket he had purchased.

"Christina, I have a surprise for you." He awkwardly shoved the store-wrapped box across the table to a spot in front of Christina.

Her first thought was, *I hope I like this*. They had been married six years, but Gerald still did not understand her tastes. She removed the wrapping paper and saw the department store label on the box. She preferred small, arty shops. She opened the box. It was a gold (probably brass) locket, the fake antique style—not really something she would select for herself, but it was okay. She was determined to avoid hurting his feelings by criticizing his choice of birthday gift, particularly since he hadn't bought anything for her last year.

"That's really sweet of you, Gerald. Thanks."

"Happy birthday! I hope you like it. Norma thought that you would. She spotted the lockets at Bullocks and thought that they were beautiful, so I bought one."

Christina was trying not to be irritated that a woman old enough to be her mother was picking out her birthday present. "Oh, it's fine. I'll put a picture of Kaylin in it." Christina was sure their three-year-old would glow with pride seeing her tiny face in that locket. Gerald sensed that Christina was not all that thrilled about the present, but he decided not to push the issue and deal instead with the growing problem of Christina's unhappiness with their marriage.

"I know you haven't been very happy about us for the last few months. I keep trying to figure out what you want. Do presents and evenings like this make you happy?"

Christina wished that he hadn't brought up this subject. She didn't want to complain when he was clearly trying to please her.

"Honey, I know you're working at making our marriage better, but what I want isn't necessarily gifts and evenings in restaurants."

Gerald tried to suppress his annoyance. He felt like an archer aiming for a target, but every time he shot his arrow, the target suddenly was moved. "Well, what *do* you want? I thought *this* was romance."

"What I want is free. Just show me that you love me in little ways every day."

"I don't know what you're talking about. We don't fight. I give you my paycheck. I do lots of things with Kaylin. What's the problem?!"

Here we go again, Christina thought, *The same old argument. One of us must be dense but I can't tell which one of us it is.*

Christina and Gerald have the same discussion over and over again. They keep missing the solution because they communicate in a vague way. Christina keeps saying she wants *love* and

Gerald keeps giving *his* version of love. Before they can even hope to unclog the statement, "I want love," they need to tell each other *what actions* would express what each considers love to be.

The Action Request: "Videotalk" in Your Living Room

Using the *action solution* means identifying and communicating the actions you want a person either to stop doing or to start doing. If support was what you were after, to translate your feelings into action equivalents, ask yourself these questions: If he were being "supportive," what specific tasks would he do? If you could see a videotape of your partner being supportive, what would you see on that tape?" I call this idea "videotalk": translating your vague complaints or general requests into the clearly defined actions that would create the change you seek. Complaints made in action terms (*action complaints*) are part of the action solution. Clear requests are *action requests*.

Christina could have gotten what she wanted from Gerald by using videotalk—identifying particular gestures and actions that helped her to feel loved. For example: "Daily loving acts for me are things like. . . hugging me when you come home, asking me about my day, interrupting me to kiss me while I'm doing the dishes, telling me you think I'm cute or beautiful, and saying that you miss me when we've spent the evening apart."

Betty was upset when she discovered that, once again, they had not set aside money for quarterly taxes. Betty had a job with an insurance company and her taxes were withheld from her paycheck. But her husband Terry worked as a free-lance business consultant and, although he made a good income, he was a poor financial manager. He never remembered to put money away for quarterly taxes—which self-employed people must pay—even though he knew Betty would get upset. She would usually end up borrowing money from her parents to rescue Terry and bail them out of the difficulty.

Betty had just attended a workshop I had given on solution-oriented living and decided to try using action terms with Terry.

"We always fight about money, and I know that you resent my interfering in your business decisions. What bugs me the most are the quarterly taxes. I get upset when you neglect to budget any money for the tax payments."

That statement was an action complaint. She did not say Terry was "irresponsible" or label him in way that could have added to his feeling blamed and increased his defensiveness. From there, Betty made an action request: "I would like you to put 25 percent of each check you get for your consultation into a savings account. In trade, I will agree to overlook my other money complaints as much as I can stand to."

Terry knew this was not going to be easy, but he also hated the constant struggle over money, so he agreed. Betty was able to pass up opportunities for the other conflicts about money now that she was not struggling frantically to pay Terry's taxes at the last moment.

Sometimes clients tell me they just can't translate their complaint into action terms. That's when the "point to it" method can save the day. When no actions come to mind, or the actions are hard to describe (such as a voice tone), try pointing out what you do or don't like *when it happens*.

Marianne was getting increasingly frustrated with her twelve-year-old, Tara. The girl "had a mouth on her," according to Marianne. But when Tara would ask what her mother was upset about, Marianne would say, "your attitude." We talked about how she might literally point to the behavior she wanted her daughter to change.

When Marianne and Tara were visiting relatives for Thanksgiving, Tara asked to go out for the evening with her older cousin, Nicole. Marianne knew that Nicole had recently been arrested for drunk driving. She was not comfortable with Tara being out with Nicole, so she said no. Tara launched into a tirade about her mother's unreasonableness, her failings as a mom, and how "put down" Nicole would feel. A red light went off in Marianne's head and she answered, "When you call me a bad mom and say I don't care about Nicole's feelings, that is what I call 'mouthing off.' " Normally Marianne would launch into a defense of her own character. When Tara did not get the usual reaction, for once, she was silent. Tara finally understood what Marianne was saying about the mouthing off. She still wanted to go out with Nicole and still asked again, but she spared her mother the usual attack on her motives and character.

The Action Compliment

While we can all point to the things we don't like in order to lessen them, we can also point to the things we *do* like and want to have happen more often.

Greg and Linda were not on the verge of divorce, but they had come to see me just to get things "back on track" since their sons had left home. Twelve years earlier I had helped them through a real crisis. Now they were struggling with grouchiness toward each other and both felt ignored and neglected.

I assigned them the task of pointing out the times either of them used playfulness and humor to solve the problem that they described as "feeling ignored" by the other. Their old pattern of getting the other's attention was to feel hurt and withdraw from each other. I wanted to establish a new pattern of light-heartedness.

In the next session Linda reported an incident they experienced while shopping. Greg was walking six paces in front of her, ignoring her. In the past she would have been angry but not told Greg what was bothering her. This time, as they passed a pet store in the mall, she said, "Wait, Greg! Let's run in here and get a leash so that you can keep track of me while we're in the mall." Greg was amused and said he liked that response much better than the quiet fuming that had been her pattern in the past.

Greg then reported how, a few days later, he had shoved his face between Linda and her magazine to say, "Whatcha doin'? Wanna go for a walk?" Before, Greg would have been hurt that she was so self-absorbed and not spending time with him, but instead he tried being cute and Linda responded favorably.

Acknowledging what we *do* like works well with everyone—not just spouses.

Gloria was aware that, at work, she rarely let anyone know what she was thinking. Even when her secretary did things that she really liked, she only said, "fine." Gloria was having lunch with me when we talked about the overall lack of enthusiasm in her department. I suggested that, rather than focusing on the lack of enthusiasm, she might start noticing what she did like and start pointing out those things to her employees.

Two months later we had lunch again and Gloria mentioned that she had successfully implemented the pointing-out-what-you-like idea. She said it was as if her staff were scheming to see how much they could please her! She was very satisfied with the change and everyone in her department seemed much more positive toward her.

Request Denied: Alternatives to Stalemate

The women I've discussed so far had partners, children, friends, and co-workers who cooperated, once things were made clear to them. What do you do when the other person says "no way" to your request. There are three potential alternatives:

> Change the translation by returning to the vague term such as "love," "support," or "responsibility" to translate that term into a new action the other person is *willing* to do.

Compromise—each giving a little.
Decide not to take any action in that area for a while—
    shelve it temporarily.

Change the Translation

Marcia and Bert had been married for ten years. Marcia's chief complaint was that Bert was not as romantic as she wanted. I asked her what "romantic" would look like in videotalk. She said, "He would hold my hand as we walked around the shopping mall or put his arm around me in a movie." Bert had always thought that "PDAs" (public displays of affection) were disgusting, so he said he could not agree to touch her romantically in public. I asked Marcia what other romantic actions Bert could do that she would like, and she said he could bring her whichever kind of flowers was on sale at the grocery store when he came home on Friday nights. Bert was willing to do this. The store was on the way and he did want to show his love, just not in the public-touching way Marcia wanted. So, by choosing the second alternative, they were able to agree upon a mutually satisfying action translation of "romantic."

Compromise

Choosing a new action for a vague complaint may involve action changes by only one party in the interaction. Compromise means that both do actions a little differently than they might have wanted.

Sheila was irritated that, once again, she was going to have to fight with Bob about visiting her family. Sheila had grown up on a farm and was very close to her parents and two sisters, who lived in a rural community forty miles outside of town. This time, rather than Sheila attacking Bob for not being close to *his* family the way Sheila was with hers, or Bob discussing why Sheila was so codependent and tied to her family's apron strings, they just focused on actions.

"Exactly how often do you want to visit your family?" Bob asked.

"I think once a month would be just fine," Sheila said.

"Well, I only want to visit them three times a year. Could we compromise and visit them every six weeks and agree *not* to talk about what it means when I don't want to go and you do?"

"I would like that much better," Sheila said. "So far, all that has happened from those discussions is that we end up feeling further and further apart, when what I really want is to feel closer to you." Sheila noticed that Bob visibly relaxed when she agreed to the compromise. His shoulders, which had been hunched up towards his ears, loosened and his face lost its tight, hard look.

Shelve It

Looking for alternative actions and reaching compromises usually lead to results in the families and couples I have worked with, but sometimes, even with a third party mediating, no agreement is reached. I have found this to be the case most often when the issue is whether or not to have a baby. You cannot have a baby for a while and see if you like it; a dog is not an adequate substitute; and you can't have just part of a baby. Typically the woman wants to have a child and the man objects. With these couples I begin by trying to see if there are ways they can handle the husband's objections. For example, if the husband's greatest worry was that their standard of living might drop because the wife might want to stay home, she could promise to keep working. Or, if the concern was that they would stop traveling, which might have been important for them, they could make agreements about vacations. If that doesn't work, I go to the third option—shelving the problem. I ask the couple to agree not to talk about the issue for three to six months, instead focusing on making their relationship stronger and more enjoyable. Working on positive aspects of a relationship usually strengthens a couple's bond, making them both more open to compromise in the long run.

Changing Action Patterns

Using action words to make requests, complaints, give praise, and reach agreements for alternatives and compromises is a powerful tool in all relationships. *Changing action patterns* is the second part of using the tools of the action solution. *Patterns* are behaviors and interactions that you do over and over again, either in many relationships (individual patterns) or in one specific relationship (dual patterns).

Marge was upset to find herself subjected to the same lecture from her partner, Jill, that she had gotten from her boss just yesterday. At work her boss informed her that she needed to be more responsible and get her business receipts turned in sooner. Marge knew her boss was right, but she would rather clean the toilets in Grand Central Station than do paperwork. At home, Jill was lecturing her about writing checks without making sure there was money in the account. "Am I surrounded by anal people, or what?" Marge quipped.

If you find yourself hearing the same message in several settings (work, friends, family) or hearing the same complaint from partner after partner, then you know you are receiving feedback about an *individual pattern.* You don't *have* to change the pattern—you may decide that you want to do things the way you always have—but if your life is turning into an emotional traffic jam, perhaps change would be good.

Changing Individual Patterns

Marge knew that her pattern was one of procrastination. She procrastinated organizing the receipts her boss wanted and keeping the check register current at home because it was boring. Since both fronts were asking her to change this pattern, she decided to comply by creating a different approach that worked for her as well. She instituted a reward system for herself. She scheduled both of the paperwork activities before meals. Twice a week on the home front, if she got her checkbook caught up in time, she and Jill would go out for dinner; if not, Marge would cook. At work on Fridays, she would organize and turn in her receipts before lunch; if she got the job done, then she would eat at a nice restaurant—if not, fast food and back to work within thirty minutes to finish the job. She succeeded in changing her individual pattern, stopped getting the annoying feedback that she was irresponsible, and started enjoying the feeling of "taking care of business."

Like any habit, the more Marge practiced, the less conscious the choice to get started had to be and the less emotionally charged it was for her. Several months later Marge was still keeping up with her paperwork, so we can be fairly certain that she has changed her pattern for good. Marge had recognized that maybe it wasn't everyone else who had a problem—perhaps it was *she* who needed to change. Marge did not wait until someone else said, "You *have* to do this or else!" She provided herself with consequences and held herself accountable, without wallowing in blame and labels (although secretly she still liked the label of anal to describe those around her).

Samantha also had an individual pattern that reared its destructive head in relationship after relationship. Initially she thought it was just a coincidence that Paul and Dick, who were her former boyfriends, both had complained about her being possessive, but now Dan was complaining too. She was twenty-eight, a competent, attractive woman working successfully in a small data management company. She should be over this jealousy stuff by now, she thought. Whenever Dan was talking on the phone, Samantha had to know who was on the other end. If he had lunch with a female co-worker, she would get upset and ask a dozen questions about the woman: Was she married? Any kids? What did she look like? She definitely needed to change this pattern.

She came to me for therapy. Together Samantha and I planned alternatives for her possessive, jealous pattern. Since one of the reasons she grilled Dan about co-workers was that she was afraid of losing him, I suggested she might try sticking with that feeling rather than moving on to accusations. Dan was able to respond to Samantha's telling him how much she loved him and didn't want to lose him. When Dan was not being treated like an immoral creep, he was able to put his arms around her to tell her he loved her.

Samantha also decided to inject some fun into the situation by exaggerating her fears to a ridiculous level. She would say in a playful way, "I suppose you had sex on the table and the waiters were riveted." Often, just joking with herself about how much she could exaggerate her fears interrupted her suspicious patterns of behaviors.

Changing Dual Patterns

In a dual pattern you find that you have a problem pattern only in one relationship. For example, if you have had several relationships where money issues were never a problem, but then you found yourself having fight after fight over money in one particular relationship, that would imply that this dual pattern occurs only in the environment created with that partner.

To change a dual pattern three things need to happen. First, you need a clear picture of what comprises the pattern—who does what, when and how, and what are the consequences? Second, you need to identify what *you* do in the pattern. Third, vary your part of the pattern until you find something that works better.

While Samantha's individual pattern recurred in many relationships, Rachel's problem was a (relationship-specific) dual pattern.

Rachel had lived with two other men before she moved in with Patrick. Rachel and Patrick had established a pattern that was not characteristic of any relationship she had been in previously.

Sorting through the mail she had just gotten out of their

apartment mailbox, Rachel noticed an envelope with no return address. It looked like one of those when-you-care-enough-to-send-the-very-best cards. She held it up to the light, but quickly scolded herself. *I've never been this way before! How could I reach such a low point that I'm to trying to see inside sealed envelopes?!* Rachel knew the answer. No one had ever cheated on her before. A year ago she had discovered that Patrick was seeing someone else when he was out of town. He said he was an idiot and that it would never happen again, but it was hard for Rachel to recover. She found herself worrying about where he was, whom he was meeting for lunch, and who was sending him a card. Maybe the card was from his mom. She sometimes sent cards.

Rachel's usual pattern when she felt suspicious toward Patrick was to withdraw; she would have confronted her previous boyfriends. But with Patrick, she just couldn't. After a few days of brooding silence she would erupt in anger, accusing him of having another woman on the side. He would deny it, give her evidence to the contrary, and things would be better for a while. Now, card in hand, she decided she didn't want to go through that pattern again.

The day the card came, Patrick arrived home at 5:45. Rachel said, "I've been stewing for the last hour about this card you received. I find myself feeling insecure and unhappy because of what happened last year. Normally, I would try to keep this to myself, but that just makes me miserable."

To her surprise, Patrick said, "You're always welcome to open my mail. I didn't know that bothered you. Here." He handed her the envelope. Rachel was relieved to see that the card inside was a joke card from Patrick's sister.

Both Rachel and Patrick changed their pattern. Rachel didn't spend days nurturing her angry feelings and Patrick, rather than acting defensively, as he had in the past, immediately reassured Rachel by letting her know he did not have a secret life.

Sometimes it is easier to see individual or dual patterns in romantic relationships, perhaps because the media encourages us to think about those kinds of relationships. Work relationships have the same kind of pattern difficulties.

Jeff's doing it again! Mary thought angrily. *Here we are in a business meeting and he is interrupting me, like always!* She maintained a calm exterior as they sat at the table in the conference room, discussing the marketing plan for the new line of products. But she *was* annoyed. Jeff is a co-worker; he is not Mary's boss and she had discussed this with him before.

Just three weeks ago she had gone into his office, closed the door, and said, "Jeff, I have a problem to talk to you about. I feel you don't treat me with respect when we are in meetings with the marketing team."

Jeff looked surprised and hurt. He had said that, particularly because he was the father of two daughters, he believed in treating women equally and he wanted to help women succeed. "I really can't imagine what you are talking about. I think you are a great member of the team and I even tell other people that."

Mary immediately felt she was being unreasonable and said, "You're probably right. Maybe I'm just being too sensitive. All I am asking is that you try to be a little more supportive when we are with the rest of the group. Okay?"

"Of course, Mary. I want to be supportive."

Looking at this latest incident, Mary realized that *his interrupting her* was what upset her. She had two action choices. First, she could give Jeff this information or, second, she could change *her* part of the pattern. Mary usually yielded the floor to Jeff—or to any other man, for that matter—who began talking in the middle of what she was saying. One of her options was to *continue talking*.

The week of the conflict with Jeff, Mary watched a very helpful television program of a panel discussion. The woman panelist had been in the corporate world for a long time. When a man tried to interrupt her, she just kept talking. Mary realized that if she did this regularly with Jeff, the frequency of his interruptions might decrease. She experimented with this new approach for a month and found that, indeed, Jeff did interrupt her much less—and she felt better about herself in general knowing that she could "hold her ground."

Pick Any Change

If you have an individual pattern or a dual pattern to change in any part of your life, ask yourself, "What can I do instead of what I usually do?" Could you be funny? Could you just be quiet, if that isn't your pattern in the first place? Could you make a request? Think of any alternative way you might respond to the situation that allows you to change your part of a pattern.

What works great in one relationship may be a total flop in the next relationship. In our next example, Zoe had a pattern that was successful in her first marriage, but was damaging in her second marriage.

From the tense interactions that had gone on the night before, Zoe knew that she and Nathan were in for a spat. This was a second marriage for both of them. Nathan believed that being able to have an argument to clear up issues was part and parcel of a good relationship. In Zoe's first marriage fighting had led her husband to withdraw from her for days at a time. With him, she had learned that it was not safe to bring up issues, let alone argue openly. Although it did seem productive to clear up issues with Nathan, it was very hard for Zoe to have the courage to stay in the room when Nathan was upset with her.

That evening, Zoe arrived home first and began cooking dinner. She noticed her hands sweating as he came through the door.

"We have to talk, Zoe," Nathan said as he put his briefcase down on the kitchen floor.

"I know we do, but it is just so hard for me." Zoe noticed a place in her neck tightening as she began to talk.

In the past Zoe avoided Nathan's confrontations by listing

reasons why she couldn't talk then: she had something else she had to do later, she was too tired, or she just did not want to talk. The excuses were plentiful.

This time was going to be different. She was going to stay in the room even if it felt overwhelming for her. Nathan brought up his frustration that Zoe had too many expectations about what he was supposed to do with her during his recreational time. She had not been happy when Nathan had chosen to join a men's basketball league at the YMCA, but she had not directly told him she objected. Instead she had avoided him and been cold on his basketball evenings. Nathan knew Zoe was upset and had gotten increasingly angry that she would not talk about what was bothering her.

This time, Zoe was able to stay put and deal with the conflict that they had over his league night. They reached the compromise that they would do something special one night a week to make up for their evening apart. Although Zoe continued to prefer not to have conflict, she discovered that by staying present with Nathan and listening to his feelings, she could fight with him without any drastic consequences—in fact, the honesty usually brought them closer to each other.

Two Fall-Back All-Reliable Patterns

Women's magazine articles that have titles such as "Ten Things to Say to Your Boss" or "Five Ways to Jump-Start Your Husband" tell you exactly what to do. Although I want to give you broader tools, I will tell you about two powerful patterns I have found in many relationships: one is the pattern of *acknowledging* the other person and the other is the pattern of using *humor*.

Acknowledging: Worth a Thousand Words

In running a business since 1975 and working with countless couples, I have found that when arguments start to escalate, one of the ways to dissipate the negative energy in the situation is by *acknowledging* the other person's viewpoint. You can acknowledge a different position from your own by restating the other person's point of view—not agreeing but letting her or him know you are listening and comprehending.

Lynn and her mother Barb were about to have their usual disagreement about Lynn's childhood. They saw their mother-daughter history together from vastly different perspectives. Barb thought she had been too strict with Lynn; Lynn thought Barb had been too preoccupied with her own life to be an attentive mother. Barb called my radio show to get some ideas about how to deal with Lynn. I suggested that she quit defending herself as to what kind of mother she was or was not and instead experiment with saying, "You were disappointed by how unavailable you felt I was when you were a child." In this statement Barb is not agreeing that she was unavailable, but she is acknowledging Lynn's feelings.

Barb later sent me a card, telling me that she and Lynn had far fewer fights since she had begun to develop the action pattern of acknowledging Lynn's position.

Humor Can Be the Best Medicine

Using humor rather than criticism can be an excellent way to change a troublesome pattern into one that nets positive results in a relationship.

Maria, a caller on my radio show, told me how she used humor to solve her problems of being ignored by her husband. Joe was working in the garage on a project that seemed to be taking most of his free weekend time. Rather than complaining, as she had done in the past, she decided to go out to the garage and have a conversation with her car. She had a cute sporty car that she liked very much.

She walked right past Joe and his workbench and strolled over to her car, embracing it as best she could. Then she said, "Hi, darling! Did you miss me? How's my little darling toy? I'd love to take you for a drive. Maybe we could go for a ride in the country. I know this great little park where we could have a nice picnic lunch together." Though Joe stood with his back to her, she could see his shoulders quivering up and down as he tried to suppress his laughter. Finally he turned around and said, "Okay! I get the point. Give me a chance to clean up and we'll go have some fun."

The handy point about patterns is that you can change a whole unworkable pattern by doing one single thing differently. Be funny, be creative, be quiet, be talkative, be lively, be sedate—but don't do what you've been doing or you will get what you've gotten.

Action Mentors

When a client comes to me feeling that she cannot possibly *be* like someone else she admires—a friend, a husband's friend, an older sister, a boss—I point out that the person she admires is not perfect. Look at her actions. Usually the behaviors are what anyone could do. Observing and doing those actions is the other way I have used the action solution in my own life and with the women I have influenced.

In my life, using other women as models for the kind of woman I would like to be generally meant going outside my tiny family for examples. I did not have older sisters or aunts and grandmothers who lived nearby. I admired my mother, particularly after I became a mother, but I learned many things about different actions women could do by observing and talking to older women.

When I was a young woman, three women taught me some actions that I still use. I had a friend named Wanda who was fifteen years older. She was very organized and kept an orderly house. I learned about making lists, organizing closets, and keeping things simple from her, and those skills have helped me organize my home and run my business.

Lynn, a neighbor, taught me how to be a relaxed mother.

She was a hippie in style, married to a professor. They were both very easy-going as parents. Since I was an uptight, worried new mother trying to be perfect, it was helpful to observe Lynn's actions. If Louis, her three-year-old, got a cut, she just washed it off rather than running to the emergency room. If dinner fell on the not-so-clean floor, she just picked it up and served it. Now, I did not completely abandon my battle against germs, but I did realize that I could be much more relaxed and the children would still survive.

My friend Sharon was a great public speaker. When I watched her make presentations, I learned about teaching. I was amazed when I saw her start a presentation to a group of clergy by asking them what counseling problems they usually encountered. I would have been afraid they would discuss some problem I was not prepared to speak about.

Kate was another friend from whom I learned action solutions. We were graduate students together. I observed how she solved problems by finding new ways to think about each situation. I noticed the questions she asked about issues that were raised in class. From her, I learned how to think more clearly by imitating the thought processes she demonstrated for me.

Notice the women who are doing things *you* would like to do but, for whatever reason, aren't. It's not that they are somehow geniuses and you are not; they have learned to take certain actions in certain situations. You can learn these actions, too. Observe them, talk to them, come straight out and ask them how they do certain things. If they make great public presentations, ask how they go about preparing. If they seem calmer than you, ask what they do to stay so peaceful. We all have different characteristics to begin with: some of us are more easy-going in temperament; others more extroverted and socially comfortable. And on and on. The point is to notice women who embody lifestyles you seek, who naturally display characteristics that you desire but with which you are unfamiliar. These women are undoubtedly performing actions that you, too, can perform.

SOLUTION-ORIENTED ACTIONS
Principles and Pathways

Action complaint principle ▪ Translate what it is that you *do not* like into action language.

In a relationship (with my boss, my partner, my friend, my child), what is something that bothers you about the other person (selfishness, jealousy, pettiness)? What actions would you see on a videotape if you saw a video of this person acting that way (videotalk)? Ask that person to stop those actions.

Action request principle ▪ Translate the general category of what you would *like* into the actions you request of the other person.

What actions would a person be doing if he was being the way you want him to be (loving, supportive, encouraging, helpful)? Ask that person to do those actions.

Action alternatives ▪ If the person you have asked to do an action refuses, you have three choices:

1. Change the translation: If the action requested is unacceptable, find an alternative action that would fit the general category of what you want.
What other actions are in that category? Ask the person if he or she would be willing to do that action.

2. Compromise: If the action requested is unacceptable to the other person, is it possible that the two of you could meet halfway?
What action or sets of actions could you and the person with whom you are negotiating find that would let each of you get some of what you want?

3. Shelve it: When you and a person with whom you are negotiating get stuck, try putting the issue aside and working on other aspects of the relationship.
What issue may need to be dropped for a while in a work relationship or at home? What other things could you work on together that would strengthen the relationship?

Changing action patterns ▪ We get into patterns of actions that we repeat with others. These are like relationship dances. Change your action and it will force a change in the pattern.

Are there patterns of action I need to change, regardless of who I am interacting with? Is there an action pattern that only happens in one relationship? What could I do differently?

Acknowledging ▪ Many interactions can improve when each party in the exchange feels that he is heard.

Is there any situation in my life now where I seem to go round and round in the same discussion? Could that situation be improved by my acknowledging the other person's point of view? Do I need to ask the other party to acknowledge my point of view?

Using humor ▪ Most situations improve with humor.

Is there some way you could inject humor into a situation, through either what you say or what you do?

Action mentors ▪ If there is someone whom you admire, think of what actions she does and do those actions yourself.

Are there action patterns and strategies that someone else does in his or her personal relationship or at work that I might adopt?

Four

The Dreaming Solution

*I*N GRADE SCHOOL learning to read had been a great challenge for me. I was a mediocre student in high school and had to have math tutors a couple of times. In spite of these extra efforts, I never received an "A" for a semester grade until I went to college. Two events turned my school performance around: first, being away at college where I realized for the first time that this was my life and I had better make it work. My father had been well-known locally. He had had one of the first radio call-in shows in Kansas City and had written twenty-two books. People would often say, "You are so lucky to have Lofton Hudson as your father." I agreed. This specialness, however, created a "Lofton's-only-child" identity for me that granted me worthiness without any effort on my part. Being away at college, out from under the shadow of my father's success, made me realize that this was *my* life. It didn't matter what my parents had accomplished; it didn't matter that my high school principal had told me that I wasn't college material; it didn't matter that my IQ scores were way above average, but my performance was consistently average or even below average. It was up to me now to make my life good or let it flop.

The second event that changed my life was learning how to do self-hypnosis as a student. Recently I read that mastering self-quieting skills, such as meditation and self-hypnosis, helps people who have been diagnosed with Attention Deficit Disorder. I am certain that, had this label been a popular diagnosis at the time (instead of underachiever), I would have been diagnosed as having ADD. (My mother said I never walked; I always ran.) Learning self-hypnosis was crucial to my success in college and has remained a valuable resource to this day. Becoming friends with my unconscious mind was my solution and I want to describe it for you as one of the solutions you can use.

In 1993 I published a book called *Making Friends with Your Unconscious Mind: The User-Friendly Guide.* This chapter is a summary of those user-friendly methods, which help you get in touch with your unconscious mind. Most likely, your unconscious mind tries to get in touch with you all the time. Dreams, physical symptoms that don't seem to have any obvious origin, and slips of the tongue are all indications that your unconscious may be trying to reach you. My goal in this chapter is to give you the means to create a productive two-way communication.

Self-hypnosis and imagery are a hair's width away from daydreaming. To simplify things, I refer to all these processes as dreaming. Dreams during sleep are a particularly powerful avenue of unconscious communication, because there is absolutely *no* interference from the conscious mind.

There are four ways to become friends with your unconscious and create a dreaming solution for yourself:

> Self-hypnosis,
> "Chatting" with your unconscious
> Meditation
> Dream interpretation

These methods may seem strange to you, but after trying them, I think you'll find them as practical and midwestern as I am!

Self-Hypnosis

When I went to college I was sure I was going to flunk out. Just before Thanksgiving, I called my father and dejectedly announced, "I'm not going to make it." He remained calm and said that when I was home for the break, I could see a doctor friend of his who specialized in hypnosis.

When I went for the session with Dr. Roland, I discovered that I liked the feeling of being relaxed. I was just an average hypnotic subject, but I decided to try it back at school. By the end of the semester that I thought was going to be a disaster, I had mostly "B's," my first "A," and only one "C." I had actually just missed the dean's list! Maybe I was not going to flunk out after all.

Self-hypnosis did some crucial things for me. First, I was able to daydream (imagine) success. If you have never gotten good grades, never had a report card without the phrase ". . . not living up to her potential," and never provided your family with the chance to rave about your performance, then it is hard to imagine exactly what that would feel like. Hypnosis and self-hypnosis let me imagine what success *would* feel like.

Second, I was able to give myself suggestions about study habits. Good students are able to concentrate. Self-hypnosis involves heightened concentration. Learning self-hypnosis taught me to concentrate and use my study time efficiently, leaving me free to have fun when my work was done.

Third, self-hypnosis was crucial in helping me manage the test anxiety that had set in after twelve years of poor test performance.

These three abilities I developed in applying self-hypnosis to my course work made it possible for me to receive my college diploma "with honors" and then to get into graduate school. In fact, after my freshman year I never received even a "C" again, except for statistics. (I guess even self-hypnosis can only do so much.)

By now I imagine you might be thinking: *This sounds scary. Could I even do self-hypnosis, if I wanted to? Could I harm myself? I'm certainly not going to let anyone else know that I am doing weird stuff like this!*

Let me assure you that if you wanted to avoid being in trance, it is much too late! You have probably been in trance while reading this book. What that means is that you have been really absorbed (I hope) and focused on what you were reading. We go into trance all the time. If you've ever been so engrossed in watching a movie that you did not hear someone call your name, that was a trance. So is driving the familiar route you travel daily, barely noticing how you got from one place to another. Being so absorbed in a lecture, a church service, or a conversation that you are unaware of the time is a natural trance. The unpleasant experience of being called upon in school and having no idea what the teacher was even discussing is also a trance state.

After experiencing hypnosis during my classes on self-hypnosis, people report a wide variety of responses. Many say their hands felt different—tingly, heavy, light, or even a pleasant sensation of lack of awareness at all of their hands. Most report that they felt much as they do when they are daydreaming, which is a natural trance. Some have noticed trance feels similar to the concentration they feel when they pray. Almost all the people in the class report that they found the experience to be pleasant, reassuring, relaxing. Each of us experiences being in trance in our own unique way. You will probably feel relaxed and you may have some of the different bodily sensations I've mentioned. Also, you are very likely to be absorbed by the thoughts, images, and memories inside your mind.

Beth was very leery about being hypnotized. She had been raised in a conservative religion and had been told that hypnosis provided the opportunity for the devil to "get in." Even though she no longer believed that, it still made her nervous.

I said, "If you are that concerned about it, then I want you to do two things. First, I want you to keep your eyes open rather than closed, so you can see everything that goes on in the room. Second, we could draw a cross on a piece of paper and you could keep that in your lap while we are doing hypnosis."

"Crosses are Catholic. That would make me just as uneasy."

We settled for the eyes-open plan. After ten minutes of hypnosis Beth chose to close her eyes anyway.

When I finished my usual ending of the hypnosis time ". . . and you can begin to come out of trance and orient to the room at your own pace and own speed," her speed was none too fast.

"That was not bad at all! I felt great. In fact, I didn't want to come back to the room."

This didn't surprise me, since that is what most of my clients and students say. Hypnosis or self-hypnosis feels refreshing and relaxing. It's great for stress reduction.

You may be wondering, what is hypnosis anyway? We know that hypnosis is characterized by heightened concentration—brain waves show us that. The sounds in the environment become less important, but are usually still heard. Memories and images are more easily available. In hypnosis, you are more open to suggestion. That quality might scare you if you were letting someone else do this for you, but since you are doing this to yourself, there is no need for concern. Occasionally people don't remember what happened in trance, but that is much less likely to occur on your own without a hypnotherapist to suggest that you will not remember.

Self-hypnosis students sometimes complain that they fall asleep. If that becomes a problem, do your self-hypnosis sitting in a straight-back chair during a time of day when you are the least likely to fall asleep.

Sometimes people hear outside noises while in hypnosis, but more often they ignore them to the point of not hearing them. When I do self-hypnosis, I suggest to myself that hearing sounds will only deepen my trance. Using this suggestion helps the noises increase the trance rather than distracting from it.

The sensations you feel may change as you go into trance. Many people in trance notice interesting sensations in their hands, as I mentioned earlier. Personally, as I go deeper into trance, I have less and less awareness of my body. Sometimes, I have experienced a very pleasant sensation of "pure spirit," a total lack of body. (This is particularly helpful to me if the reason I was going into trance was to relieve a symptom of illness.) Self-hypnosis is like the experience of lying in bed awake, but very physically relaxed, while your mind is active, as in daydreaming. I have often found dozing in the back of a car on a long trip to be a very trance-inducing experience—that is, feeling very relaxed physically yet and focused mentally.

The experience of trance is a highly individualized experience. You cannot "do it wrong." While you should be aware of what you might expect, I hesitate to describe trance in too much detail, because I want you to simply enjoy *whatever* you experience.

Creating Your Own Custom-Made Trance

For over twenty years I have been the director of a counseling center where most of the staff members are trained in hypnosis. One of our staff members was preparing a speech on self-hypnosis he was going to make before a local organization. He asked each of us how we induce self-hypnosis. One common principle for us all was to take slow, deep breaths.

Generally, relaxing and just "letting go" help create a trance. If you have never consciously tried to relax, try this technique: tense up your body as tightly as you can and then release all your muscles at once. Tensing and relaxing sections of your body progressively—for example, one leg and then the other; one arm and then the other—helps you to experience the difference between tension and relaxation. (If you have been to Lamaze classes, this will be familiar to you.)

I am going to give you three specific ways to go into trance. But experiment with what I describe until you arrive at your own favorite method, your custom-made trance. I had one client who found that she could go into a deep trance only while taking a warm bath. On very rare occasions, clients have reported that they absolutely cannot close their eyes and relax. In these unusual cases, I suggest either going for a walk in a familiar place or sitting in a rocking chair. The point is to discover whatever works for you in creating your own trance. As you practice, you will be able to vary where and when you go into trance. At this point in my life, I can go into trance in practically any setting, just by closing my eyes and breathing deeply.

During self-hypnosis, you may want to make the suggestion that you will get better and better at going into trance each time you practice. Like any skill, the more you practice, the better you become. Before you come out of trance, say, "The next time I go into trance, it will be even easier and more enjoyable."

Here are three easy methods for going into trance:

> The relaxing-place method
> The muscle-group method
> The eye-roll technique

Relaxing-Place Trance

To use the relaxing-place method, begin by taking three slow deep breaths. As you breathe in, imagine breathing in peace. As you exhale, imagine breathing out tension. You might say to yourself, *Breathe in peace; breathe out tension.* You might imagine the inhaled air being a soothing blue color, while the exhaled air containing the tension might be red. Or you might imagine the peaceful air being cool and the tension air being hot.

Now imagine being in a relaxing place. You could pick the woods, the beach, or sitting in front of a fireplace. I asked one client what the most relaxing place would be for him, and he said the cockpit of a plane. That would not have been my first choice! It was his, however. Remember, whatever works for you *is* what works.

As you imagine the relaxing place, recall the sights, sounds, smells, and feelings of the environment. Be creative and fanciful in designing this special place for yourself.

Margo was a ten-year-old girl who said that her grand-mother's backyard was the most relaxing place in the world for her. She described it generally; then I used my imagination to describe it in some detail for her as she went into trance. In my amplifications I included *sights, sounds, smells* and *feelings*.

I said that she could notice the lacy pattern of the sunlight on the ground as it shines through the trees and the greenness of the leaves and the grass *(sights)*. . . . She could notice the clouds floating lazily in the sky *(sights)*. . . . She could notice the smell of the dirt, of the mowed grass, of the plants in her grandmother's backyard *(smells)*. . . . She could listen to the sounds of birds, the breeze blowing gently through the trees, the lawn mower off in the distance *(sounds)*. . . . She could feel the soft breeze through her hair, the warmth of the sun on her face, or the cool dampness of the grass under her body (feelings).

Because Margo needed help with physical problems (stomachaches that had no medically identifiable cause), I went on to make suggestions about feeling peaceful inside and her body functioning perfectly.

As I say these things, I talk slowly and in a soft, monotone voice. This change in voice tone and speed is not "on purpose," but a result of my having entered into a trance with the client.

Often the word *imagery* brings to mind visual experiences. Some people are not as visual as others, so their daydreams contain more sounds or feelings. If sounds are more relaxing in creating your trance, then focus on sounds and minimize sights. I find the sound of rain very trance-inducing; others find music entrancing If you are more auditory than visual in your daydreaming, you might emphasize the sounds of the breeze in the trees or the sounds of water to get relaxed. If you find that bodily sensations affect you the most, use images of temperature or other physical sensations. For example, you might want to imagine feelings of water in a warm summer stream; the coolness and freshness of the clean sheets when you first get into a freshly-made bed; the warmth of the sun as you rest on a shore.

If you feel uncertain about going into trance for the first time, you could initially make an audiotape for yourself. You could use the following script from my book, *Making Friends with Your Unconscious Mind*. Record this into a tape recorder:

Take three deep breaths. As you inhale, say to yourself, "Breathe in peace." As you exhale, say, "Breathe out tension." As you exhale the third time, allow your body to slump.

You can allow any outside noises to help you go more deeply into trance, feeling more relaxed and comfortable. You can now imagine being on the beach. You may notice the rushing sounds of the waves as they come in with a roar and the soft musical sound as they ebb out over and over again. You may notice the smell of the salty water as you feel the healing warmth of the sun on your skin. You could look out over the water and notice how the ocean is different colors in different places and how the sunlight dances upon the water. You might notice the smell of your favorite sunscreen and the oily feeling on your skin. You can notice the sounds of birds near the beach and look out over the ocean. You might see a seagull catching the wind in her wings and just remaining lazily suspended in the air. You might notice the sounds of people playing on the beach in the distance or the sounds of the wind coming off the ocean. You might reach down and pick up a handful of warm sand and feel the tickling sensation of it flowing between your fingers, noticing how each grain is different. You could notice the moist warmth of the sea breeze as it lightly caresses the hair on your body.

Two other options are to make your own script about a favorite relaxing place of your own or to buy a hypnosis audiotape. I would like you to see if you can use this method without a tape first; most people find this easier to do than they thought it would be.

Muscle-Group Method

The muscle-group method, which is the first method I learned when I was taught self-hypnosis, is excellent for relieving physical discomfort and relaxing your body. If you are on an airplane or in some other situation where you feel that your body is uncomfortable, this is helpful for staying as relaxed as possible. A friend who went for a CAT scan reported that this helped her in that confining, uncomfortable process.

You may begin with the same slow breathing, again giving yourself suggestions that outside noises will only help you to relax more. Either start with your head and work down to your toes or the reverse. Tell each part of your body to relax. For example, you could say to yourself, "My big toe is beginning to relax and that relaxation is spreading to the next toe and the next until peace and relaxation fill all my toes. That relaxation is spreading to the balls of my feet and then my arch. . . ."

This method is helpful for the people who find visualization difficult. It also has a distinct advantage for people whose bodies are tense or ill. When you are concentrating on each part of your body, you can particularly focus on a part that needs attention because of an illness or injury.

Eye-Roll Trance

The third method of self-hypnosis that you might like to experiment with was developed by Herbert and David Spiegel (father and son). They have a simple three-step method:

> With your eyes open, roll your eyes up toward your eyebrows as high as you can get them. Try to see the top of your head.
> With your eyes still gazing upwards, close your lids and take in a deep breath.
> Exhale. Let your eyes relax, and let your body float.

I personally don't use this method often myself, but some of my students report that it is their favorite method because it is a short, simple, and effective method for going into trance.

Whichever method you choose, devote at least ten minutes a day to practicing it. Like any skill, you need to practice to reap the benefits. Just find a quiet place. Sit in a chair with your hands on your thighs or the arms of the chair, and begin. If you are worried about falling asleep, set an alarm for twenty minutes. Close your eyes—unless that bothers you, in which case, pick a spot on the wall to stare at—and begin breathing slowly and deeply.

When in Trance . . . Daydream

Once you are in even a very mild trance, you can use one of several methods to consider a problem and create a solution: daydreaming about the future, chatting with your unconscious, and making specific suggestions to yourself.

In spite of what your third-grade teacher may have told you, daydreaming is not bad. In fact, it is crucial. It is impossible to accomplish a task if you cannot *imagine* doing it first. Now we don't have to imagine consciously all the tasks we do in a normal day, because our unconscious stores that kind of information for us. But if we want to *improve* our performance in school, give a speech, or ask for a raise, it certainly does make it easier to accomplish if you can imagine doing it first.

Lauren was devastated by her divorce. "I had been married twenty-two years and I thought we were doing fine. I went back to my hometown with our two teenage daughters to visit my mother. When we came home, I discovered that Stan had moved out and left a letter saying that he didn't want to be married anymore. I just couldn't believe it!"

Over the next three months we worked on practical concerns, such as supporting herself financially, getting legal issues handled, and helping her daughters cope with this trying time. Near Christmas, I noticed that Lauren was becoming more and more depressed, even though she had handled everything relative to the divorce. She said, "I can't imagine that I will ever have another happy Christmas."

I knew that Lauren could not envision this Christmas being a good one, but perhaps if we picked one a couple of years away, she might be able to imagine future happiness. It was important that she develop an image of a happy future to counteract the depression and grief she was currently feeling.

I used hypnosis with her and asked her to imagine her daughters and at least one of their future boyfriends, her friends, and her family coming over for a sumptuous holiday feast at her house. In trance, she created images of everyone laughing, savoring the food, and enjoying the beauty she had created in her house. After this hypnosis session Lauren was still sad, but she also had a growing sense of hope. At least now she could imagine getting through this first Christmas alone and she knew in her head, if not in her heart, that there would be a time of happiness again. As an assignment outside of therapy, I asked Lauren to spend a little time each evening before falling asleep imagining some pleasant event in her future. Had she known about this concept of imagining future success, she could have done this on her own.

Not only can using your imagination—or daydreaming, as I prefer to call it—help with emotional issues, but it can also help with physical concerns. Medical researchers now acknowledge that patients can boost their immune systems by using imagination. Imagery on its own and in conjunction with biofeedback and hypnosis are all ways of tapping into that creative inner resource of healing that we all possess.

Hypnosis can also be helpful in managing physical responses to anxiety-producing situations. Before I was interviewed by Katie Couric on the *Today Show,* I imagined how it would feel to express myself clearly and even joke with Katie about the book I had written. When I went on the show, I was pleased at how relaxed I felt—some of which I credit to Katie and some to my unconscious mind!

Applying your imagination to the solutions approaches presented in this book can speed up your problem-solving by an easy ten-fold. The more you can imagine success, whether in actions or in thinking, the more success you will have in changing your actions and your thinking.

"Chatting" with Your Unconscious

So far I have emphasized giving ideas to your unconscious in the form of suggestions, but you can also receive ideas from the unconscious. I mentioned earlier that you can "chat" with your unconscious. There are two ways to carry on this universal type of conversation: through simple yes-no answers or receiving whole phrases or images.

Again, I know that these ideas might sound weird. Just remember that you are always in control when you are doing self-hypnosis. Over a lifetime, you have stored many actions that you may have observed others doing or that you did yourself at some time and have forgotten to continue to do. Those ideas are stored in your unconscious. You have made decisions about life that you were not consciously aware of, such as deciding not to trust a group of people based on some event. Getting these messages from within yourself about possible new ways of acting and about what decisions you made regarding the events in your life is simply something you allow to happen, not anything forced upon you.

When I first learned to do self-hypnosis in the 1960s, I was trained to signal with my fingers (small jerky twitches) to answer questions asked in trance. Movement in the index finger of my right hand indicated yes and the index finger of my left hand, no. (As the years passed, I have modified this signaling so that I only feel a tingling in my finger for the appropriate answer.) Then, in 1978, I attended a workshop on neuro-linguistic programming (NLP), a type of therapy that emphasizes working with the unconscious. There I learned that each person could let his or her body choose and generate its own signals for yes and no. For me, this is a tingling on the left side of my face. Most of my clients experience a tingling in an extremity, such as their hands or feet, but one client uses a pulsing noise in the ears to signal yes.

In order to try this on your own, first let yourself relax into a light trance. Notice your entire body drifting into deep comfort. Ask your unconscious to pick some sensation and then to increase that sensation to indicate a yes answer. Just relax and notice which sensation increases. Then ask your unconscious to increase it again so you can be sure that it is your yes signal.

Repeat this same procedure to discover your no signal. From time to time, some clients report that their no signal is the clear decrease in their yes signal. Trust your unconscious; allow it to reveal itself in its own way.

You might wonder, after discovering your yes and no signals, whether or not they will change. I found that my signals changed at first but now are routine and predictable. But that doesn't mean that they will never change again. I usually check yes and no signals before I start to ask questions. The key is to avoid superimposing your conscious thoughts; let your unconscious speak through these subtle physical movements.

In chatting with your unconscious you may talk either as if talking to yourself or as if addressing a separate part of yourself. The types of questions you might ask are: "Unconscious, are you willing to help me with this (headache, anger, procrastination)?" "Will you help me relax whenever I see my (ex-husband, boss, difficult client, etc.)?" It is possible that your unconscious might say no. For example, if you asked for help with a headache, but the headache is the only way your unconscious knows to get you to slow down, then it may refuse you. If for some reason your unconscious says no to this first request for help, just ask it to prepare to help you accomplish your goal some time in the future. It may be that there is an inner wisdom about not changing too quickly.

If you need something beyond a yes-no answer, ask for images or phrases. For example, say you asked the question, "Is there anything I need to change in order to be free to accomplish this goal?" and got a yes response, now you can imagine a blackboard or television set. On the screen or the board you can ask that a word appear to cue you about what you still need to handle. If you aren't that visual, then you could imagine hearing the word, the phrase, or the sentence. I know that this type of internal communication might sound unusual to you, but once you start practicing it becomes as normal as any daydream.

It seems to me that self-hypnosis is simply the refinement of something that the mind does anyway—daydreaming, "spacing out," talking to itself. These are all natural, inner activities. I just want you to be able to focus these ever-present abilities in a way that leads to solutions to your particular life challenges.

Meditation

People often use the terms *meditation* and *self-hypnosis* interchangeably, but actually the goals of each are very different. The goal of self-hypnosis is to *accomplish* something—create a different state-of-being that helps you make a change or acquire a skill. The goal of meditation is to empty the mind. The physiological difference between these two approaches is reflected in different brain-wave patterns that characterize self-hypnosis and meditation. Brain waves measured during self-hypnosis look like those measured when a person is in deep concentration. Brain waves during meditation look like those during a state of deep relaxation when the mind is "silent." Self-hypnosis has a definite Western flavor of *doing;* meditation has an Eastern flavor of *being.*

There are physiological benefits to meditation, particularly lowering blood pressure, and I personally enjoy the still feeling that it gives me. If you lead a hectic life with your brain in "overdrive" most of the time, try meditation. I find that the feeling I get in my body when meditating is somewhat similar to when I use hypnosis. I use meditation when I do not want to bother being creative with imagery and just want to feel more centered.

Almost all the Eastern religions make use of meditation in one form or another. Some of the more common forms of meditation, such as Transcendental Meditation, use the repetition of a word or phrase (a "mantra") as a way to empty the mind of thoughts. (In Western religion, only Catholicism uses a repetitive prayer—the rosary.) My method of meditation is very simple. Sit quietly, with your eyes closed and your body in a comfortable position. (I prefer to have my hands resting on my thighs.) Observe and slow the rhythm of your breathing and repeat a word or phrase to yourself each time you exhale. Keep repeating that word inside like a chant.

I sometimes use the word *one;* sometimes a religious word has meaning for me. Traditionally, mantras have long vowel sounds—you've heard the "OM" chant of yoga—but you can repeat any word that feels appropriate to you.

If thoughts come into your mind, casually dismiss them, telling yourself that you will deal with those thoughts later. As you increase your mind-emptying skills, you will be less and less bothered by mental chatter. I find that picturing the word written in front of me can be helpful in stilling my thoughts. The best meditative attitude is one of tolerance: Do not berate yourself for having those interrupting thoughts; just gently dismiss them until later.

Plan to have your meditation time in a quiet place and choose the length of time you will put aside for this. I recommend ten or twenty minutes a day. I find it ideal to meditate in the early evening when I first come home from work, having used ten minutes of self-hypnosis in the morning to start my day. Twenty minutes a day of meditation or self-hypnosis will give you a longer, healthier, and happier life. What an enjoyable and useful way to have spent just those few minutes!

In my many years of working with people who have self-esteem issues—and who doesn't?—I have found that one way to feel better about oneself is to do something that is challenging. Changing your habits to incorporate twenty minutes a day of relaxation or meditation can make you feel proud of yourself on two levels: first, for discovering that you have the self-control and self-discipline to take this time for self-improvement; second, reducing the stress you had come to accept as "normal."

Dreams in the Night

Night dreaming provides a powerful link to the unconscious. You dream around four times every night, whether or not you remember the dreams. If you need help remembering your dreams, use the skills you have learned in self-hypnosis. Ask your unconscious for help in remembering your dreams. As you fall asleep, repeat over and over, "Let me remember a dream tonight." Have a pad of paper and a pencil by your bed, and as soon as you awaken, write down whatever you can remember about your dream.

I use four different approaches to dream interpretation. First, you can ask yourself, "How is this like my life?" Usually the answer will be fairly obvious. Was the theme in the dream about being busy and out of control? About too much freedom or too little? Did you feel overwhelmed, rejected, fearful, or abandoned?

Second, you can pretend that you *are* each part and character of the dream to see if that helps you understand the dream. For example, if you dreamed about a car that you couldn't control, you can say, "I am a big car. The driver can't control me. I will take the woman inside wherever I want." (From this "being the car" you might look what part of you is out of control and taking you places that you doubt you should be.) Or if you dreamed about a ship, you might say, "I am a ship. People use me to get from one place to another. I am sturdy and hard to sink." (How are people in your life using you to get from one place to another and how are you "sturdy and difficult to sink"?) If you dreamed about a childhood friend, what part of you is like that friend and what, if anything, might you need to do about it?

Third, look at the language of the dream. Look for puns, double meanings of words, names that come up. If you have teenagers, the term "chill" might have different meanings for you. If you dreamed about a "dock," might that refer to a doctor or medical situation? If you dreamed about someone named "Phil," might that refer to something you need to "fill," like a void in your life?

Jolene was in a very frustrating situation. For over three years her husband, a farmer, had been having an affair with the wife of the farmer who owned the next farm. Jolene would catch her husband contacting or seeing the woman, confront him, and then he would swear it was over. Jolene told me that she didn't dream, but she wanted to come to one of my dream groups anyway, just for the fun of it. After the second meeting she reported that she had had a dream that was like a snapshot: It was the image of a flat tire. I couldn't help laughing when she said this. I said, "Jolene, I would be 'flat tired' too if I were married to Bob!" Then she started to laugh. She had tried so many different solutions—therapy, pastoral counseling, and changing the way she approached Bob. It was time to give up trying to get Bob to be faithful, and get a divorce. The vivid image of her emotional state provided by her unconscious gave her permission to move on.

Fourth, there are symbols and images in dreams that you can read about in books, but keep in mind that you know more than the book when it comes to what a particular symbol means *for you*. That is why I suggest that you ask your unconscious, through signals and self-hypnosis, if you are on the right track in the way you are interpreting your dream.

Besides writing down your dreams as they happen, you can ask for a dream about a particular dilemma you are facing. This is called "dream programming." What types of issues are appropriate for dream programming? Any issues that are important to you. For example, you might ask for more understanding about a relationship with someone or for advice on what you should do about a job. You might ask your unconscious for help on getting over some painful event.

The first step in dream programming is to apply your conscious mind to the issue. Keep a dream journal. Before you go to sleep at night, write down all your thoughts regarding the topic of concern. For example, if you want help getting over a painful relationship, write down why you should get over it. Write down what the advantages would be if you did *not* get over it. (There might be some valid reason for not getting over the problem.) Consider what purpose you think the relationship might be serving. In other words, consciously analyze the problem as fully as possible. Often this is a learning experience in itself.

Next, devise a "dream request" sentence. It could be a sentence such as, "Help me get over the relationship with _____." As you go to sleep, repeat the request over and over to yourself.

Immediately upon awakening, jot down all you can remember about your dream or dreams. Dreams seem to vanish if we don't capture them quickly. I usually remember a couple of dreams from each night's sleep and record the ones that seem most vivid. My unconscious usually makes it clear which dream is the answer to my request by having one dream stand out much more clearly than dreams usually do.

How do you know what to "work on" in your life? Most of the time I do not work on anything. I find that if there is something I need to pay attention to, it will reach my consciousness in one of three ways. I will notice that I feel upset, develop a physical symptom such as a headache, or have a vivid dream that will grab my attention. As a follow-up on a vivid dream, I first analyze it and then, if I need to find out something more, I will program my unconscious to dream about the topic again.

A few years ago I had a tubal ligation scheduled a month in advance. In the meantime, my unconscious gave me five dreams about men I had known throughout my life, with whom I had thought I might have a child. Saying good-bye to that possibility was one of the steps I needed to go through. I continued to have dreams about being a woman and what that meant for me. Finally, I realized that, even though my unconscious said I should go ahead with the surgery through the yes-no signal technique, I still felt some uneasiness. I asked my unconscious to create a dream about whatever remained for me to resolve before I had the surgery. I had a dream about a hypnotherapist who taught a relationship class. (That was what my former husband and I did together in the waking world.) The dream made it clear to me that I needed to ask him to change the way he was talking and acting about the surgery. He himself had refused to have a vasectomy and he seemed indifferent to my feeling of grief that I would never bear another child. I asked him to change how he talked to me about this. He admitted that he had been insensitive because he was afraid I would insist that he have a vasectomy, and he agreed to stop acting as if this was of no importance to me. When I asked my unconscious through the yes-no signal technique, "Is there anything else that I need to work on before surgery?" there was nothing else. I noticed I was finally looking forward to the freedom (no more birth control) the outcome would bring and the sadness I had felt about the tubal ligation was gone.

Sometimes you have applied all these great solutions—you have asked for and gotten help from your unconscious; you have changed your thinking and action patterns—but still you feel sad about the situation. The next chapter is about what to do if the only thing left to change is your feelings.

DREAMING SOLUTION
Principles and Pathways

Self-hypnosis principle ▪ Self-hypnosis is a natural state that we are in when we concentrate on anything. It is a method for getting help from your unconscious through imagery or asking for ideas.
Are there times that you have concentrated so intently on something you were doing, reading, or a conversation that you were having with

someone that you lost track of time? (That was trance.) Think of a place where you would feel relaxed and safe. Could you imagine being there now? What positive things could you say to yourself as you think of your relaxing place?

Chatting with your unconscious ▪ The unconscious can give you an understanding on a deeper level. By getting either phrases and images or yes-no signals from your unconscious, you can receive answers from your inner self.

Ask your unconscious to pick a signal for yes and no. What questions would you like for your unconscious to help you with? Could your unconscious help you get either an image from the past that might help you or an image of the future in terms of what you would like to accomplish?

Learning from your night dreams ▪ You can discover what your unconscious wishes to communicate to you by interpreting your dreams. By asking yourself how a dream is like your life, pretending to be each part of the dream, noticing the language of the dream in terms of double meanings, and identifying symbols, you can discover its meaning. You can also "program" your unconscious to have a dream about a particular topic.

What would you like your unconscious to give you more information about? Could you formulate that idea into a sentence to repeat to yourself as you go to sleep? As soon as you awaken, write down the dream and interpret it according to the guidelines above.

Meditation ▪ The goal of meditation is to clear your mind of thoughts and create a stillness inside. The body may feel similar in a meditation state and hypnosis, while the mind will be doing dissimilar activities.

Find a location in your home where you will be free from distractions. Close your eyes, slow your breathing, and repeat a word or syllable in your mind. If thoughts intrude, casually dismiss them until your meditation time (ten to twenty minutes) is over.

Five

The Feeling Solution

*D*ONNA TRIED HARD not to feel sad. Her father had died five months ago and friends were telling her that she should be "over it" by now. But no matter what her amateur-therapist friends told her, she felt sad. She and her dad had been close; they had talked a couple of times a week and she still missed him. She tried not to think about him, but so many things reminded her of him: when the leaves began to change color during his favorite season of the year; when his favorite songs would come over the speaker system at the office; or when a food that he loved would be on a menu. Donna would try to think about something else, but in spite of all her efforts, she would suddenly feel on the verge of tears, sometimes even bursting into tears unexpectedly.

I suggested that her effort to avoid her feelings was not working and that perhaps she could deliberately think about her father at a certain time every day. Donna had a long commute to work, and I thought that imagining herself talking to him as she drove to and from work would be a way for her to contain her sad feelings so that they did not spill over unexpectedly. She welcomed this suggestion, saying that it was a tremendous relief to have a "right" time and place for her grief. After a couple of months of allowing herself to acknowledge fully the immensity of her loss, she found that having imaginary conversations with him from time to time was all she now needed.

Accepting and Acknowledging Feelings

Donna learned an important principle. If you run from your feelings, they tend to run after you. Whether these are feelings of anger, sadness, shame, or guilt, the best approach is to simply acknowledge to yourself that you feel them. *Acknowledging* your feelings doesn't mean wallowing in them. It means facing them straight on, knowing that feelings are neither right nor wrong; they just *are*.

The No-Blame Way

Besides trying to avoid our feelings, the second mistake we commonly make is blaming ourselves for our feelings. A woman friend told me about the method she had used to stop blaming herself for not being perfect. She used what she referred to as her "deity chant." Whenever she made a common human error, like forgetting an appointment, she would repeat to herself, "I am not God and I cannot be perfect." Most of us would feel embarrassed by such a mistake, but in the past my friend would have berated herself for being so stupid and forgetful for several days. Five years ago she had a baby—which tends to disrupt perfectionism by virtue of sheer exhaustion— and she developed tolerance for the reigning imperfection by teasing herself with her deity chant. She said, "It's so great not to pick on myself for not being perfect!"

When you have upset feelings, why add to the distress by picking on yourself for having those feeling? Instead, try acknowledging how you feel and see if there is anything to do in the present about those feelings.

Meredith was very upset with herself for feeling as if she wanted to slap her four-year-old daughter, Heidi. I told Meredith that any mother whose four-year-old has thrown a fit in the middle of the shopping mall or screamed "You can't make me!" down every aisle of the supermarket has known that feeling of rage. I asked her if she had ever actually hit Heidi. Meredith assured me that she had not hit her and that she would not hit her, but the fact that she had felt like hitting Heidi scared her.

I helped her see the difference between *feeling* and *doing*. I said, "Feeling like hurting someone, or even murdering someone, is not the same as doing it. Feelings are not a problem. *Actions* based on feelings can be a problem, however."

I asked Meredith how she kept from "losing it" with Heidi. She seemed to have a lot of prevention plans. One was to leave the room for a few minutes. Another was to say to herself, "I am 5 feet 9 inches tall and weigh 150 pounds. Heidi is less than a yard tall and 45 pounds. I am in charge." Her third strategy was to put Heidi in her room and hold the door shut until they both had a chance to calm down. These all seemed like decent self-control strategies to me, and I felt assured Meredith would not hurt Heidi. She just needed to acknowledge how she was feeling and know that she was not abnormal.

Not all feelings that trouble us are of sadness or anger. Being sexually attracted to someone outside your committed relationship is something you have probably felt—and then berated yourself for feeling it. I always go back to the distinction I made with Meredith between actions and feelings. Feeling like being sexual with someone is not a problem; *acting* sexual or further cultivating that relationship, however, may create a problem. In my personal relationships I have found that if I tell my partner I am feeling attracted towards someone, then those feelings tend to dissolve. But trying my solution, you might want to consider your partner's history of jealousy to gauge how he or she would handle such a revelation. Acknowledging sexual feelings for others can be surprisingly helpful, but only if both partners agree that it is a natural and safe topic. Then, if those feelings continue to be a problem, you might need some outside help.

You Don't Have to Agree *to Acknowledge*

If your partner has feelings that are difficult for you to handle, such as going through a time of not feeling attracted to you,

you probably feel like running and hiding and then using denial to rewrite a less painful version of the scene. This, as you know, does not work. Instead, acknowledge the feelings head-on by saying, "I understand that right now you do not feel as attracted to me," and do the actions that are likely to rekindle attraction. Trying to force yourself or someone else to deny or alter his or her feelings rarely works. Acknowledging the unwanted feelings helps take away their "forbidden" power and keeps them out in the open instead of feeling that there's something is wrong, but not knowing what.

So often I have seen couples escalate their difficulties because the partners would not say these six simple words: "I understand what you are feeling."

Julie and Doug had been having the same fight for quite a while. Over a year ago Doug had had a one-night stand with a woman while he was away on a business trip. He felt so guilty about it that he confessed. Julie was shaken but willing to continue the marriage. However, it was hard on her and she could not get Doug to acknowledge that it must be difficult for her to trust him again. Whenever she would say that she felt insecure when he was out of town and needed him to call more often, he would say that she was being unreasonable and even label her as "paranoid." They were stalemated around this issue until Doug quit trying to invalidate Julie's fear and simply said, "I understand that you still feel scared that I might betray you." Julie visibly relaxed. He didn't insist that she stop feeling that way, he didn't say she was right or wrong for feeling that way, he only acknowledged her feelings. He also made a point of calling more often, but the crucial turning point was to stop denying Julie's right to her own feelings.

One principle to remember is that *resistance begets persistence*. The more you try to resist your emotions or someone else's, the more those emotions will tend to "hang around" as a problem. Another principle to remember is that *acknowledging a person's feelings doesn't mean that you agree with the other's viewpoint*. You probably don't think he or she is "right." It just means that you hear and understand what you are being told. The goal of acknowledging the other person's feelings is the same as when you acknowledge your own: to restrain yourself from attaching judgments of yourself as good or bad.

Rituals to Heal by

If, after facing your feelings without blame, you still feel upset, perhaps it is time to create a healing ritual.

Sara had done all the right things since her divorce a year ago. She had learned self-hypnosis and meditation; she had changed how she communicated with people to include action requests; and she had stopped plaguing herself with questions about why her marriage of thirteen years had dissolved without much warning. But she still felt sad and stuck in feeling betrayed and angry over the breakup of the marriage. Sara and I talked about how she might create a ritual as a symbolic way of putting the divorce behind her and moving on.

Sara had not seen the breakup coming. Her husband had moved out rather suddenly, leaving her completely unprepared for a divorce. She later learned that her husband had been having an affair for almost a year. She still had the I'm-out-of-here letter he had written to her announcing his departure. We planned a ceremony to acknowledge the divorce that included getting rid of that letter! Since the anniversary of the court date was coming up, something on, or very near, that day seemed appropriate.

Sara carried that letter with her night and day for a week just the way she had been carrying around the painful memory of reading the letter. Every night for a week she wrote a letter to her former·husband that she had no intention of mailing. She could be venomous; she could plead; she could cast aspersions on his character and his family. The point was to bring out into the open, and dispose of, all that Sara had had to cope with inside her head and her heart. On a night when the children were with their father, she re-read all the letters she had written and the letter from her ex-husband that symbolized the end of the marriage. (She had made a copy of this letter so that when the children grew up and wanted to know what happened, they could read it for themselves. The copy was kept at her parents' house so that it wouldn't contaminate her environment.)

She had gone to the music store and selected Native American flute music she thought would suit the occasion. She put on an old robe that she had worn often when making his breakfast. In front of her fireplace she prepared a ceremonial altar with candles and all that she had gathered for her ritual. She started a fire and burned the letters very slowly. She would put in one of the many pages and watch that page turn to black dusty ash before she added another page. Then she burned a picture of her former husband and her together on a vacation in Cape Cod during the time that she now knew he had been having an affair. As she sat in front of the fireplace watching the fire turn to smoldering red coals, she pictured the good times that awaited her in the future. She knew that she would continue to grow in her career; she knew that as her children got older, she would have more freedom and more fun with them on a different level; and she thought it likely that she would have another relationship. As she watched the smoke rising from the dying fire that represented her marriage, she was going to let those images of the future carry her forward.

Then Sara took a long bubble bath. She put candles in the bathroom and stayed in the bath until all the bubbles had disappeared. She felt that this was a way of washing away the tangled web of feelings that she had about her former husband. Sometimes she longed for him. Sometimes she had fantasies of his dying, from either some horrible disease or a debilitating accident (particularly involving the inability to use the lower half of his body!). The bath was her way of cleansing away those feelings and then continuing with her new life, fresh and clean.

The next day Sara had arranged to have brunch with two of her best friends at a swanky restaurant as a way of symbolizing her desire to get back into life in a positive and fulfilling way.

This ritual did not get rid of Sara's painful feelings, nor did it prevent her from reacting with distress to things her former husband still said that upset her. But the ritual did give her a sense of closure she would not have had without it. The ceremony changed her way of viewing the tremendous loss she had experienced; she was no longer looking backwards, but at the road ahead.

Designing Your Ritual

Deciding to do a ritual is tricky when it comes to timing. You have to wait until you are really ready to *let go*. You can't short-circuit your grief by having a ceremony a month after someone you love has died. Like the ad for wine, "Serve no ritual before its time." Start with the other solutions discussed in the earlier chapters, and if you still feel a need to do something more, do this!

How can you design your own ritual to help you in times of loss? The first step is to select a symbol. Symbols can be found in something you already own, something that you purchase, or something that you create. Something you already own could be a marriage license, a picture from a time that was painful for you, an evaluation from your boss that hurt you, a receipt from a motel—anything you possess that adequately symbolizes what you want to leave behind.

Jackie had always had an unpleasant relationship with her mother. When she was just a child, her mother would punish her for minor infractions by not speaking to her for as long as two weeks. Jackie's father had been many years older than her mother and had died when Jackie was only eleven. Being an only child, Jackie had been very close to her mother in her own way, but at the same time she felt constantly judged.

Now Jackie was in her early forties. Her mother had been dead for three years, but she still felt that her mother was watching her. Jackie told me that she still had all of her mom's things in her basement and that her husband wanted her to get rid of them. But just as she still carried her mother's judgments within her, she was unwilling to part with her mother's possessions.

I asked Jackie to bring in three items that had belonged to her mother. She selected a box of savings stamps from a company that was now out of existence, an iron, and a kitchen utensil. I suggested that she carry around the box of saving stamps, night and day, for a week and then do something with it. I told her to even carry it with her to the bathroom if she got up at night, just the way she had been carrying her mother around with her night and day, even though her mother had been dead for three years.

I saw Jackie later while I was out shopping. She told me that she had thought it was a silly idea but had done it anyway and, at the end of the week, she had sent the box to her cousin in Wyoming to be placed in the basement of her mother's house. Jackie reported that since getting rid of the box of stamps she had not felt that her mother was judging everything she did and she had been able to dispose of all of her mother's things, except for a few valuable antiques.

Jackie used a symbol she already possessed, but you can also combine something you have with something you create.

Cathy's husband, Tom, had had an affair which she had discovered when she noticed a debit for a dozen roses on his charge account. Although she had suspected that he was having an affair, the receipt stunned her with unwanted confirmation.

Tom and Cathy had separated for several months, during which time Tom became clear that he wanted to be with Cathy and that the affair had been a stupid mistake. Although Cathy was still afraid of Tom's instability, she was willing to try living with him again, particularly since they had a small child who missed his daddy.

As they resumed living together, Cathy began to sense that Tom was truly committed to the relationship. Together they decided to create a ritual symbolizing the termination of the affair and their mutual recommitment to the marriage. How would they design this ritual? Cathy had saved the receipt for the roses, and they each wrote a letter about how they felt about that time. They read their letters to each other and Tom apologized for the terrible pain he had caused Cathy. They burned the letters and the receipt, and then sprinkled the ashes in a stream they had picnicked by in the past. They repeated their wedding vows in that idyllic setting, went home and took a bath together, and finally went out to eat at their favorite restaurant.

You can create symbolism in any conceivable manner: by drawing pictures, painting rocks, writing letters, making clay statues or rag dolls. And you don't need to have any artistic abilities. One woman drew a huge spiral on a piece of paper with little stick figures to represent the demise of her marriage. She drew a hand to represent her husband slapping her; a picture of a baby to express how abandoned she felt when she had their child; a picture of coins for when her husband lost his job for yelling at his boss; a beer bottle to mark when his drinking began to get out of hand; a picture of a police car for when she had to call the police because he had become violent; and, finally, a gavel signifying the divorce.

Women's losses often center around miscarriages, abortions, stillbirths, and infertility. Using dolls and other baby items combined with letters written to the unborn child is an excellent way to express the grief for which our culture provides no outlet.

Lisa decided that buying a symbol would work best for her. She had had an abortion three years ago and still felt bad about that decision, even though, rationally, she had not seen any other choice at the time. She had been a student, and an older man, whom she was dating, had been the father of the child. He was not willing to marry her and, at nineteen years of age, she could not imagine how she could possibly survive financially on her own with a child. He had accompanied her to the clinic and had paid for the abortion, but she could not shake her feelings of sadness. She decided to buy a bib, which she carried around with her for a month. She chose a bib that said, "I love Mommy," which I thought was her way of asking for forgiveness. After giving herself the month's time with the bib, she was willing to let it go. She buried it lovingly in a special spot.

Another young woman was brought to my office by her mother. The mother said that her daughter was a great student (she was in her freshman year of college) but that suddenly, a month ago, her grades had plummeted. I excused the mother from the session and spoke alone with the girl. She told me that she had had an abortion a month ago and was feeling very sad about the loss. Her boyfriend had been very supportive and had gotten the money together to pay for the abortion, but they were both grieving. I suggested they go to a crafts store and buy a very small doll, carry it around for a week, and then have a burial for it. Having some concrete way to express her grief was helpful for her and she was able to return to her productive college life.

Unresolved losses in the area of career can be just as painful as human losses. Here, again, symbols owned or created can be used to acknowledge, express, and dissolve the distressing emotional component.

Nancy had owned a small business, employing about a dozen people, many of whom had been with her for a number of years. When her business got into financial trouble, she asked her staff to help. Some of the staff members began having secret meetings and several left the business at once. She was able to turn the business around without those staff members, but she still felt upset and betrayed.

She had heard me give a speech on using rituals to help resolve painful events and she decided that she would create one for herself. She included her secretary, Mary, who was also her close friend, because Mary had also been very affected by what felt like a betrayal. Nancy and Mary had photos of all the staff. They decided to burn the pictures, one at a time, as they talked about each person who had left and how they felt about that person. Afterwards, they walked to a nearby creek and sprinkled the ashes in the water, and then went to Nancy's yard and planted a small tree to commemorate their "growing the business" together. Each step of this ritual provided a release of painful feelings *and* the creation of a nurturing, productive future. They were able to put this episode behind them and move on, once the full range of their feelings had been honored.

All these women, whether dealing with grief around a relationship, the loss of a child, or a business crisis, chose to do a ritual as a way of dealing with unresolved sadness. However, rituals can also be designed in response to anger.

A woman in her thirties came for therapy because she was tired of being angry about sexual abuse that had been perpetrated by her stepfather. He was dead now, but the memories of his violations haunted this woman, inciting a chronic state of anger in her. She had confronted her mother for not protecting her, but her anger had not dissipated.

The main way he had abused her was by watching her through keyholes and coming into her room while she was dressing. To symbolize this constant invasion of her childhood, she drew a picture of a keyhole with an eye looking through it. I suggested that, after burning the picture, she complete her ritual by taking a special bath and writing a letter to herself, affirming that she would not let anyone violate her again and that she deserved to be loved and cherished. She liked this as a way of completing her ceremony.

To recap: the first steps in designing a ritual include identifying the unresolved issue and choosing the appropriate symbol by creating it, buying it, or choosing it from items that exist already. Then you can decide to get rid of something by burying it, burning it, flushing it down the toilet, putting it down the disposal, throwing it into a lake, ocean, or river—whatever means matches best your feelings of getting rid of the difficulty. One divorced woman I know made a point of putting her marriage license under the large concrete slab that she had laid for her patio.

It may be that you want to take something *in* instead of, or in addition to, getting rid of it. Like the woman who had been abused by her stepfather, who needed to incorporate good feelings about herself and what she deserved, you may want to include some symbol of incorporation in your ceremony. Maybe because I was raised a Baptist, I always like to include *washing away* as part of the ceremony. Putting candles in the bathroom and taking a bath or a shower, or swimming in the ocean or a stream, always seems a perfect way of symbolizing a fresh start.

Another special touch to a ritual is to have a celebration with friends or family. They don't even have to know that this is the end of a ceremony for you, only that you want to have a nice dinner or meal. For you—as it has for me—it can symbolize going back into life.

Ritual Replenishment

The rituals I've mentioned so far are used to deal with the negative in our lives. But women also need rituals to *replenish* themselves. I have been frantically busy for most of my adult life. Having four children and a career, going through a divorce and then creating a stepfamily, ten years later facing a second divorce, running a small business, taking care of aging parents—the demands are literally unrelenting. One of the ways I manage not to "lose it" is by doing small things that replenish me. I do self-hypnosis daily for ten minutes; I incorporate little rituals into my daily routine, such as having lunch with friends, listening to music while I clean my office, playing the piano at least three times a week, working out, and reading books on

religion or mysteries. I think of all the everyday activities as
rituals of replenishment.

One woman I know puts as many replenishing rituals into
her life as possible. Little things, such as having an attractive
place to open her mail while drinking her favorite herbal tea,
taking bubble baths, surrounding herself with potpourri, and
meditating every morning before her family wakes up are all
ways she enriches her life and sustains her feelings of well-being
within herself.

Ritual Connections

Steven J. Wolin and his colleagues have studied families who
had a member with a severe drinking problem. They have found
that families who managed to keep their rituals intact, such as
Sunday dinner, Thanksgiving, and religious holidays, did not
define their families as alcoholic families. Families whose rituals
were disrupted by drinking thought of themselves as alcoholic
and were more likely to have alcoholics in future generations.

As individuals, couples, and as families, keeping rituals of
connection intact creates a sense of stability and a sense that
there is order in your universe. Connection rituals can be activities such as going to church on Sundays, reading the paper
together on Sunday morning, having cinnamon rolls on Saturday at your favorite restaurant, or walking in your favorite park.
All these create stability in your life. Whatever rituals help you
feel that there are parts of your life that you can count on,
do them.

So many women live lives of sacrifice for others. I certainly
don't condemn that, but I think that even if your goal is to give
to others, you have to know how to give to yourself so that you
don't "bottom out." Other people can revive you with the love
and caring they give you, but ultimately it's best to be in charge
of your own replenishment. When you are primarily dependent
on someone else to bring you pleasure and comfort, it is like
sitting at a banquet table that is covered with your favorite
foods, waiting for someone to feed you because your hands are

tied behind your back. Certainly the pleasure you get from relationships is very important, but you must also be able to recharge your own battery.

During one of the painful times in my life, I was determined to practice what I had preached about using rituals to restore my feelings of stability and protect myself from all the chaos that seemed to be brewing around me. My aging parents were having major difficulties, my husband moved out, I had to stop my radio show, and my youngest child needed almost more than I could give—or so it felt. During that dark time, I listened to some lively African music, worked out regularly, went back to church, and reconnected with some old friends. I did all the things I could think of to keep myself centered. It worked! I managed to make it through that time with a sense that, at my core, I would have the power to restore myself, no matter what happens.

FEELING SOLUTION
Principles and Pathways

Accept and acknowledge feelings ▪ Trying to directly change your feelings or someone else's feelings is difficult. It does help to acknowledge your feelings and avoid denying them.
Are there feelings that you try to avoid? Could you acknowledge to yourself or to someone else that you are having those feelings? Notice the effect of that acknowledgment.

Rituals help heal feelings ▪ Designing and carrying out rituals for a painful or angry event can help heal feelings. The symbols and actions that you choose can demonstrate leaving something behind or having a funeral for those feelings.
Is there something that you need to resolve? Assuming you have done the practical things necessary to resolve the issue, such as leaving a painful situation or confronting someone who hurt you, could you now select a symbol for that event? What would be the most appro-

priate way for you to rid yourself of that symbol (burying, burning, tearing in little pieces)? Is there some way you could celebrate the ending?

Rituals can replenish ▪ Build rituals into your daily or weekly routine that comfort and support you. These can be taking the time to have a favorite herbal tea, lunch with a friend, going for walks—whatever regular habits (rituals) you can develop for comfort and replenishment.

What do you now do that replenishes you? Could you do that more often? Are there other ways you could build enjoyment and comfort into your routine, such as listening to your favorite music when you are opening your mail? Are there things you do on a weekly basis that replenish you, such as attending a religious service or meeting a friend for breakfast on Saturdays?

.. II

Putting Solutions to Work on All Fronts

Six

Partnership

WHEN I TALK ABOUT RELATIONSHIPS, I usually mean romantic sexual relationships. I tend to give examples from heterosexual couples only because that is what I have had the most experience with as a therapist and as a woman. In therapy and among my friends, these concepts have been applied to lesbian relationships as well.

In thinking about the most common complaints and concerns I have heard from my women clients (and personally experienced as well), several themes emerge:

> How to get out of a cycle of fights and arguments
> How to get the male partner to talk at all
> How to decrease critical communications from a partner
> How to increase love and closeness
> How to leave the past behind
> How to stay put in your relationship, even if it does not improve but you do not want a divorce
> When to leave

Anne and Dean found themselves stuck in a cycle of endless fighting. They owned a small business together (it was a second marriage for both of them). Dean's twenty-five-year-old son Mark was involved in the business. Mark tended to take advantage of his privileged position as the son of the owners by coming in late, sleeping in the store rather than driving home when he became too drunk at a bar located near the store, and speaking disrespectfully to his stepmother. Dean felt guilty about not having been around when Mark was younger because Mark's mother had custody, so he tolerated more than he should have. Anne was annoyed at Dean for allowing Mark to get away with so much irresponsible behavior, particularly in front of the employees. She would find herself starring at Dean with an are-you-just-going-to-let-that-pass look. Anne and Dean had reached a point where they could not talk about Mark without getting into a fight.

Anne used all four types of solutions. First, realizing that her attempt to get Dean to see her point of view was not working, she decided to use an action request. She asked that she and Dean each write out what they expected from Mark in concrete terms, such as getting to work on time, saying hello to Anne when she came in the store, and not using the store as a crash pad. Anne and Dean were able to agree on specific points regarding how they and Mark conducted the business. Anne agreed to stop harping about what Mark had done in the past. Simply agreeing on what constituted the bottom line worked. They also agreed that Mark could not continue to work for them if these simple requests were not followed. This was their action solution.

Second, Anne wanted to stop reacting with such distress whenever Mark was around. His mere presence annoyed her. She used her unconscious and practiced putting herself in trance (the dreaming solution) and breathing deeply. She told herself that whenever she saw either Dean or Mark at work, heard their voices, or thought about either of them in regard to work, she would breathe the way she breathed in trance. She found that, if she could control her physiological response to her husband and Mark, she could keep herself from getting upset and saying things that provoked Dean into another round of the same fight.

Third, Anne made a point to stop obsessing over whether

Dean loved her or Mark the most or why Dean and Mark behaved in this allied way. It was easy for Anne to think in terms of Dean's dysfunctional first marriage as the root of this and other evils. Instead, Anne focused on what she could do differently in how she thought about Dean and Mark. This was the thinking solution. Dropping the nonproductive "why" questions and their related labels, she began to ask "how" and "what" questions that led to positive actions. Anne thereby decreased her role in upsetting herself by her futile self-talk.

Fourth, Anne used the feeling solution in two ways. First, she asked Dean to acknowledge that Mark did, in fact, refuse to speak to her in the store. She had not asked for this previously, but had felt that her point of view was not acknowledged because Dean would just change the subject or keep talking whenever she would bring this up. When she directly asked for acknowledgment, Dean had no difficulty in acknowledging Mark's refusal to speak to Anne. Second, she decided to spend a little time on herself. She had a full-time job in addition to their business; she had not had even a moment to do any of her replenishment rituals that relieved stress and helped her to feel centered. She went back to her aerobics class, took special time for herself everyday to meditate, read her favorite magazine cover to cover, and made a point of having lunch once a week with a friend. Her life had become nothing but dealing with the conflict about Mark; by re-instituting rituals that soothed her, she was able to regain a better balance.

Like so many women in relationships, Anne tended to take on the full responsibility for fixing the relationship. Whenever I have been in a marital crisis, I am always the one who initiates therapy and takes a very active part in trying to make a difference. With few exceptions it seems to me that we women tend to be the keepers of relationships. Is there a simple solution to this? I don't think so. But awareness of this imbalance in advance and agreements about how you will handle the difficulties when they arise may help.

The Talking Solution

Many woman complain that they do not know what their partner is thinking or feeling. Deborah Tannen, a linguist, would explain this particularly gender-related trait by saying that men don't want to be in a one-down position and therefore don't admit to feeling weak, scared, or fearful. Discussing language differences is one way to explain why men and women behave differently. But, again, answering the question why does not lead to solutions to these relationship difficulties.

Couples typically get into patterns in which one does all the talking and the other is the strong, silent type—or even the weak, silent type. If you yourself are stuck in this particular pattern, don't despair. Men, language difficulties or not, *can* be shown the benefits of self-expression.

As we considered in the actions solution section, think about times when you have been able to talk clearly and smoothly with your partner. What was going on then? Were you taking a walk together? Were you on a trip in the car so that there just wasn't anything else to do but talk? Was it after sex? Was it in a restaurant? What is the context that leads to your best talking times?

Heather and Jim found that, with two preschoolers at home, they simply rarely talked. When they did, Heather carried the conversation. However, they discovered that when they put the kids in the car for the two-hour trip to Grandma's, the children became so interested in the sights that they finally had some time to talk and Jim, without television and duties to distract him, talked more. (If the trip had been longer than two hours, you know the phrase, "How much longer till we get there?" would have put Jim and Heather in the funny farm!) Then, when they were visiting grandma, Heather and Jim would have a couple of hours alone, thanks to Heather's mother's willingness to entertain the grandchildren.

Besides looking at what *settings* are likely to foster more talking, you can also start to notice if there are actual *barriers* that prevent talking. The television is mentioned most often by my clients and friends as a main deterrent to communication.

Keri and Tim had been married for ten years and Keri complained that she just couldn't get Tim to talk. He would fixate on the sports channel and virtually become a piece of furniture in the family room for most of the evening. Keri complained to Tim about the situation repeatedly, but found that she just couldn't get anywhere with him. She saw that her part of the pattern was to complain and continue to ask Tim to change. She came to a class I offered and decided to change her part of the pattern. She began going out in the evenings and spending time with friends. Naturally, this was much more fun than watching Tim watch television. Tim became worried that she was going to find someone else. Keri was attractive and fun-loving, and I think she would have found someone else rather quickly if Tim had not faced the possibility of losing her and realized that he had to change. He began going out with her at night and restricted his television to Monday night football and one other night. He invited her to rent a movie on her way home every Wednesday that they could watch together. Most importantly, *he* said that they needed to talk more and asked her to spend half an hour at night talking to him about how their workdays had gone and anything else she was willing to share.

Breaking the Fight Cycle

Keri and Tim were lucky compared to many of the couples I've seen in therapy. They could speak a civil word to each other. Some couples cannot communicate a single sentence without having the conversation escalate into a battle.

I was counseling a couple who would plummet into a vicious argument as soon as the session began. I vowed to break this pattern, not only to help them but to relieve my own stress from dealing with such a volatile couple. First I introduced the action solution by suggesting that when things started to escalate, one of them take the initiative to ask the question, "Do you have a request?" Once they grasped the concept of videotalk, making a simple request statement would bring them back from irrational and unproductive sputterings to identifying what actions they each wanted and how to get those actions.

I was also concerned about their fights at home. I suggested they do something absurd each time a fight started: go into the bathroom, whereupon the husband was to sit on the toilet and the wife was to stand in the tub! This strange behavior was a way to jolt them out of their pattern of escalating sniping.

If action solutions do not stop the arguing with your partner, you may need to remember that all you can really control is *yourself*. Learning to relax rather than tensing up in these times of conflict is one method you can always apply. Simply (or nor so simply!) breathe deeply whenever you see, hear, or think about the person and the conflict to reduce your reaction. Removing your part of the escalating war dance is, after all, half the battle.

Sometimes outright fighting is not the problem so much as a pattern of hurtful or critical remarks. I have repeatedly encountered this problem in my relationships. Perhaps being an only child did not prepare me to deal with people, who claimed to love me, speaking meanly to me. However, I did learn some ways of handling this unwanted pattern that involve the action solution.

In my first marriage, when my spouse would say something that was critical, I would do one of two things. I would withdraw into myself—not as a punishment, though; in fact, if it had been intended as a punishment, it would have failed because there was no sign that he noticed my withdrawal!—or I would try harder and harder to please, thinking that if I could just be a better wife, neater, more efficient, then I would not incur the criticism. Those responses did nothing to curb his critical remarks, and after a while I started to resent struggling so hard to please him.

In my second relationship, after a few years of tranquil living I was shocked to hear the same tone of voice and harsh put-downs that I had heard in my first marriage. This time I was smarter. I would immediately say, "Please don't use that tone of voice with me," or, "If you have a request, that is fine, but I do not want to be labeled in that way." (This was an action solution that focused on nonverbal actions.) My comments worked much better than my withdrawal had in the past. I no longer felt hopelessly stuck in a struggle to please, nor did I allow the criticism to go unnoticed. If you are going to try this approach, be aware of your voice tone as you respond, so that the love you feel for that person will still be present in your voice while you are holding him or her accountable for the remark.

Love, Like Any Flower, Needs Water

Many of the issues I have discussed so far involve clearing up the problem areas. Once areas of conflict have been resolved, love can re-emerge spontaneously, but it is also wise to think about ways of creating more love. Essential to this pleasant challenge is learning what you and your partner view as manifestations of love. If tender touching means love to you, then you had better be sure that your partner knows that. If talking and sharing thoughts and feelings is part of love for one of you, then there had better be time for quality talking in your relationship.

Scott and Stacey came to see me for the sole purpose of increasing the closeness in their relationship. More often, couples stop in for a quick session when they are halfway to divorce court. Creating a fulfilling marriage is much more difficult when the marriage is already in a crisis. Scott and Stacey were wisely acting before the trouble had gotten out of hand.

Scott was the romantic one, loving picnics, calls at work, and funny cards. Stacey seemed more the rational, organized backbone of the family, making sure that efficiency was created in most activities. They both felt ignored and unappreciated.

The first solution for them was the thinking solution; they quickly grasped the idea that no one definition of loving behavior is the absolute, true, and *only* definition.

The second solution concerned the actions of love they each wanted from the other. I suggested that they each think of three loving things they would like the other to do. Scott wanted Stacey to call him at work, to plan a surprise outing, and to "stop vacuuming for once and give him a hug." Stacey wanted Scott to arrange for the wallpaper to be hung in the family room, to help clean up the dinner dishes, and to clean his whiskers out of the sink in the morning. This new pattern worked so well for them that they developed the habit of asking each other every morning, "What can I do for you today that would be love for you?"

Sometimes it is helpful to go back to things you used to do that increased your feelings of closeness. When you were first in love, did you spend more time in bed talking? When you felt the closest to each other, were you away together on vacations? Maybe even an overnight in a local hotel might bring back some of those intimate feelings. Examine what worked in the past and try those activities again.

"Unfinished Business"

Oftentimes the reason that love and closeness are not flourishing between you is because of painful past events whose effects are not fully healed. An affair, a big disappointment, a betrayal of some sort, might be the reason that your relationship cannot get back on track. The first step is to talk about what happened and make agreements about the future, so that the wound will not be re-opened. It might take months, or even years, for the trust to build enough to heal the wound.

Holly and Mike had been married for over thirty years when Holly had an affair. Mike was devastated. They came to therapy to rebuild their marriage and to ensure that such a violation would not occur again. The therapy had been over more than a year when Mike and Holly scheduled an appointment. Holly was irritated that Mike still felt upset around the time of the anniversary of the betrayal. I reminded them that I had mentioned the use of a ritual to symbolize the final step in recovering from this event. They remembered the suggestion but had never done it. Now, they agreed, it was time. They selected a symbol of that awful time, burned it together, and composed new wedding vows and said them to each other. The symbol they selected was a picture from Holly's workplace, since that was where the affair had started. Mike told me some months later, when we ran into each other at a workshop, that this ritual completed the healing for them. They now felt their relationship was deeper and stronger than it had been, even in their best times.

The Challenge of "Staying Put"

Sometimes women want to stay married in spite of some negative quality in the relationship that makes it chronically difficult. A woman may not wish to raise children alone; the financial loss might be too great; or her partner has become disabled and she does not want to abandon him.

My close friend, Lily, applied three solutions to her marriage with Eric. A relationship difficulty had arisen that probably warranted leaving, but she did not want to give up. This was a second marriage for her and she was committed to keeping this marriage intact. Lily used the dreaming solution of self-hypnosis to center her, the feeling solution of creating a ritual to help heal the relationship, and action solutions to create a new present and protect the future.

In her marriage to Eric, Lily dealt with infidelity and pregnancy at the same time. The week Lily became pregnant, Eric began an extramarital relationship that Lily did not discover for four more months. This was totally unexpected. Lily had imagined that people would have affairs when the relationship was not great, but not when things were wonderful. In Eric's first marriage, his wife had done the same thing to him, so Lily had also believed that he would not betray her, given the effect the betrayal had had on him. Eric came to see that he was more infatuated with his ideas than with the other woman and that he was about to make the worst mistake of his life. Lily was determined to make it through this devastating event. She refused to give up and began applying the four solutions to her own relationship. She did not go for therapy, which left some issues unresolved and patterns unchanged. She avoided therapy for two reasons: Eric did not want to go and, because she felt so embarrassed for herself and for him, she could not bear anyone else to know. Lily's unconscious became her therapist and guide in her healing process.

With the dreaming solution, Lily used self-hypnosis to deal with what had happened and to guide her healing. The physical stress of the painful event and the emotional stress of forgiving such a betrayal were lessened by the soothing effects of trance, which she combined with her spiritual resources of prayer.

Next Lily suggested that, as a couple, they create a healing ritual. Eric agreed. Together they wrote a letter to the woman, asking her to stay away from Eric. Lily also wrote to her about what it is like to go through a divorce and hoped that the woman would be more protective of her own marriage. Lily and Eric burned the other woman's picture and her letters to Eric after mailing their letter to her. They bathed each other as a symbol of washing away what had happened. Finally, they repeated their vows. Lily would not claim that this ritual ended her pain, but it was helpful in reaching another phase of healing.

Action-wise, Lily and Eric focused on what needed to happen in their relationship now and what they would do in the future if he were tempted again to have an affair. He agreed to tell Lily if he felt strongly attracted to another woman and they would deal with it as a team, not alone. Lily had done this in her first marriage, at a time when she was feeling romantic towards another man, and it had helped preserve their relationship for some years. When people are able to keep their word and approach the relationship as a team, these strategies *do* save marriages.

When Do *You* Give Up?

In many cases the breakdown of the marriage is not caused by obvious offenses, such as an affair, alcohol or drug abuse, or violence, but by the *absence* of some quality that is important to one partner but not the other. In one of my relationships, the issue was an inability to achieve the closeness I craved. I tried filling up my life with women friends to make up for the lack of intimacy, and that did help for a number of years. I also tried therapy, and that again delayed the breakup for another year or two. But eventually we both reached a point where there was just too big a gap between what we each wanted in a relationship. Nevertheless, the actions of finding other ways to fulfill your needs can help preserve your relationship, if that is what you both want.

When *do* you then give up on a relationship? I would say that there are two factors that will determine ending a relationship. The first is unwillingness, which is often difficult to distinguish from lack of ability, to do what is necessary for a relationship. This might be due to a lack of skills or to a lack of commitment to the marriage. Examples of unwillingness are if a spouse tells you something—such as a career move to another city—is very important, but you are unwilling to accommodate your partner. Or, if you repeatedly tell your partner that you are scared by his or her tone of voice, but there is no noticeable attempt to modify it, that would be either unwillingness or lack of ability to change. The second reason to leave a relationship involves violations. These usually imply a lack of ethics and include lying, sexual betrayals, physical abuse, mismanagement of money so that it threatens financial stability, drug or alcohol abuse, or excessive gambling—some act of unethical or dangerous behavior. These are discussed in chapters 9 and 10. If the violating party seeks help then there is hope, but without acknowledgment of the violation there can only be further difficulty.

Sarah and Chuck had been together for sixteen years. They had married right out of high school and, in the course of the intervening years, had taken very different paths. Chuck was a mechanic and Sarah held a professional position. When they came to therapy, Sarah was the one wanting change; Chuck just wanted to be left alone. The therapy focused on skills that seemed fairly elementary—communicating in videotalk, spending pleasurable social times together, and not name-calling—but Chuck did not make any lasting changes because he was not committed to the marriage. It would be hard to say if he could not, or would not, make changes, but he steadfastly refused to do anything different in his relationship with Sarah. She became more creative and inventive about her part in their pattern, but eventually she lost the energy to keep pulling the relationship forward a centimeter at a time, and divorced Chuck.

If repeated attempts at improvement do not yield results, and if trying to fill your life up with substitute satisfactions fails, you may feel compelled to give up. Maybe it *is* time to move the game. Do all you can, but don't be a dope about it! I rarely advise couples to get a divorce unless there is violence in the relationship, because I consider that drastic decision to be theirs. I think you have to look in your heart, weigh your alternatives, and find out the answer for yourself. I know the circumstances that have compelled me to leave: both times, on some level, I felt that I would not survive if I stayed in the relationship. In my first marriage I became so depressed and lost so much weight that I looked like a walking skeleton. A betrayal in my second marriage left me physically ill for nearly two years. When it happened again, I felt that my physical health would be at stake if I did not get out of that marriage.

After my second husband told me in July of 1994 that he wanted to divorce me, we still had over a dozen teaching engagements through March of 1995, where we would have to appear in public, teaching couples how to create good relationships! This was something I dreaded, as you can well imagine, but I felt an obligation to keep my word to those sponsors and to keep in mind that the principles we taught were very valuable when people are motivated to improve or save a relationship.

When someone is dead set on leaving, there are only a very few things you can do about it. It is often hard to accept the reality that you can't force someone to have a relationship with you.

One of the ways I survived that horrible time of teaching people how to have good relationships, while standing next to someone who was unwilling to have one with me, was to use self-hypnosis. Through self-hypnosis I was able to avoid reacting negatively to my husband. I imagined that he was only an actor made up to look like my former husband and that I was surrounded by holy light that would protect me from any destructiveness he was going through. The dreaming solution helped me survive.

Giving up on my marriage was very hard for me, particularly the second time. When I was single between my two marriages, I had put much thought into what could make a relationship work, so I assumed I had made a wiser choice. Nevertheless, I *am* certain about the four elements required for a relationship to endure:

Commitment—staying even when times are tough
Skills—videotalk, resolving conflicts, showing affection, all those things that help you resolve the
day-to-day problems of living with someone
Humor—if you can't laugh about it, then you know
you are in trouble
Ethics—you can't have a relationship with a liar, because trust is the basis for love.

In spite of the challenge of writing about relationships in the
midst of the end of a very important one for me, I think that
we are meant to be with other people and that a satisfying
relationship, while not essential for happiness, does add to one's
contentment.

I also think that parenting is something that adds a unique
kind of breadth and depth to your life. Delighting in my children and applying solutions to the role of being a mother has
been an adventure for me during the last quarter of a century. I
hope you will experience greater delight as a mother through
the application of solutions to motherhood in the next chapter.

SOLUTIONS FOR PARTNERSHIP
Principles and Pathways

Teach each other what a good relationship is ▪ Communicate videotalk of a successful relationship to your partner.
*What do you want in a relationship? Teach your partner what a
great relationship would look like.*

Use your unconscious to modify your reactions ▪ If you need to modify how you respond to your partner, then use self-hypnosis to
control your responses.
*Do you find that you get too easily "hooked into" a conflict? Put
yourself in trance and tell yourself that whenever you see your spouse,
hear him, or think of him, that will be your signal to breathe deeply
and be calm.*

Fill up your life if your relationship is lacking but you wish to stay ▪ If
a relationship is lacking, but you do not wish to leave, create
compensations.
*If you are lonely or need more from a partner who seems incapable of
giving more, could you have same-sex friends that would compensate
for some of the friendship needs that are not being met? Are there
other ways you could care for yourself that would make up for what is
missing in the relationship?*

*Leave if there are continued violations or out-of-control behav-
iors* ▪ If a partner behaves in an unethical, dangerous, or abusive manner, you may need to leave the relationship.
*Do you find that you have repeatedly excused or forgiven your partner
for violations? Has your partner refused to get help for his difficulty?
Does his problem put you or other family members in danger? Do you
need to protect yourself and your family by getting out of the relationship?*

Seven

Parenting

*T*HERE HAVE BEEN TIMES when my career hit stellar
peaks. There have been times when an intimate relationship has thrilled me. But nothing has ever gratified me to
my bones the way parenting has. I have four children: two
launched, one on the launch pad, and one in grade school.
Parenting has stretched me, overwhelmed me, touched me, and
taught me. Working with parents who were having parenting
problems taught me, too, but the impact of dealing with children—face to face at home—was always more profound than
reading a hundred articles or counseling a hundred families.

The most challenging time for me was the single parenting
(although being the biological parent in a stepfamily opened
new dimensions of conflict I had not anticipated). I doubt that
many women who are single parents will have the time to read,
so if you have friends in that challenging situation, tell them all
you can about the solutions you think they could use.

As I thought about the problems I have faced and observed
what other mothers face, they seemed to fall into clusters:

> The first cluster is trying too hard or giving up too
>   easily.
> The second is setting rules and enforcing consequences.
> The third is getting cooperation from the other parent,
>   if there is one.
> The fourth is dealing with maternal guilt.
> The fifth is coping with grown children.

Trying Too Hard ... Giving Up Too Soon

When you first become a mother, trying too hard is usually the biggest and most common problem. I had had little exposure to babies before I became a mother, so I read all I could and hoped that I wouldn't make any serious mistakes. The fear of motherhood was probably compounded by the fact that my father, who was a therapist, would tell me stories from therapy about parents who had said something that ruined the child for life—something to the effect of, "You can never do anything right." The child, I was told, grew up to be a street person!

I confess that I did not dip my first baby into bath water for the first five weeks of her life. She would protest when I tried, so I would just wash her off with cotton balls one little part at a time. (I really had a thinking problem—the incorrect notion that babies should not cry.) My own mother seemed even less confident about this process than I was. (She had the same thinking problem.) Five weeks following my delivery, my mother came to visit me and help with the baby. We prepared the bath water, as I had done before without completing the task, and Mother went into the bathroom with the baby. After half an hour she had still not washed the baby. She was as chicken as I was! I decided that was that. I had to *just do it*. I marched into the bathroom and took gentle command of the situation—and have been confidently bathing babies ever since.

After reading so much about babies while I was pregnant, and then experiencing the full reality of a living, breathing, wailing baby, I came to a conclusion that I hope will help anyone who is about to have a baby. Instead of doing a thesis on child care based upon what experts tell you, pretend you are in the jungle alone with your baby. What feels like the natural thing to do? Now it may be that your first instinct is to go to a hotel and have a good night's sleep, but I mean the instinct *after* that! Most new moms are overloaded with mountains of advice from well-meaning relatives and friends about how to be a good mother. Listen less and trust your instincts of love and nurturing more. (I hope *trusting yourself* is a message you have gotten from all the solutions in this book.)

I loved having babies. I loved being part of their discovery of the world. Seeing the day through their eyes was so magical. Crumpling a dry fall leaf for the first time, seeing the moon for the first time, discovering language—I would not trade a minute of it. Then things became more challenging. Those magical creatures have opinions!

Once those opinions intrude, the problem for some mothers becomes not trying too hard, but giving up too easily. This sense of defeat is particularly likely to occur when the child becomes a teenager. It is hard to find a balance between letting go and having boundaries when your child is about to become an adult.

Setting Rules . . . Enforcing Consequences

One of my sons made getting ready for school an ordeal. He was in first grade. The mornings became a battle ground and "Hurry up!" the battle cry. I began searching for a change in this pattern. A friend suggested that I turn the mornings into more of a game. I made a "ticket to breakfast." Each corner of the ticket had a task to complete before coming to breakfast: take shower, get dressed, put away pajamas, and comb hair. (I assisted on this last one.) He could have breakfast—and even watch cartoons during breakfast—if he completed his ticket. This creativity shifted the morning from a battle to a game and the problem disappeared. After a month or so the tickets were dropped, but by that time the routine was well established.

In between the magical moments of connection with your child are the hard parts of parenting: deciding what rules to make, and then getting kids to follow the rules. My second child, Nick, was a brilliant orator when it came to debating about the appropriateness of rules or consequences. Discussing a new rule with him left me feeling like I had just come through a Gestapo interrogation! (He has become a loving adult, a good friend, and successful musician, but I often think he would have made a superb trial attorney.) Mr. Hindalong, his sixth-grade teacher, once remarked, "When Nick and I have a private discussion about a conflict we have had in class, I end up thinking, 'Maybe I *am* Hitler!'"

Nick helped me learn an important principle of parenting and a true pattern change for me. *No child can make your lips move.* Just because that child wants to discuss the justice, or lack thereof, of your demands and compare them to the prevailing standards in his or her friends' homes, it does not mean *you* have to respond.

Before I had children, I studied behavioral psychology. I had thought long and hard about which behaviors I would reward and which ones I would either ignore or eliminate by delivering a negative consequence. It amuses me to hear graduate students who don't have children talk the same idealistic way I did about the prospect of parenting. It sounds so simple in the lab with the rats and the mazes. In the house with the two toddlers, nothing is simple—especially trying to "shape" behavior.

Action requests are essential when talking to children about their duties and responsibilities. Saying to your teenager, "I want you to be more responsible," is not half as effective as saying, "I want you to get your homework done and turned in every day." As mothers, you need to unpack the contents of those mysterious boxes labeled with vague words like *responsible* so that your children know what the boxes contain—what action is expected of them.

One family who came to my counseling center had lots of conflict with their teenager. Since he was not in any serious trouble, we used videotalk to clarify what the parents wanted. One of the things the parents wanted was for their son to clean his room. They made an agreement with him that he would remove all dirty laundry from his room, put away his clean clothes, and change his sheets by 4:00 p.m. on Saturday or he would not get to go out over the weekend. To my surprise, as everyone got up to leave, the mother said, "But I want him to *want* to clean his room." My co-therapist responded, without missing a beat, "I am forty-four years old and I still don't want to clean my room. Let's just get the actions we want and see if those feelings emerge later. I don't think people this age are likely to *want* to clean their rooms." I suspect the mother was a little disappointed: she not only wanted a clean room; she wanted a miracle!

The Lows of High Expectations

One source of struggle in some families is the pressure of high expectations of what a teenager or even younger child can and will do. The first child is more often the victim of unreasonably high expectations because the parents haven't been properly "housebroken." I used the thinking solution in examining my thoughts about expectations, limits, and consequences. My guideline for keeping in check my own responses to unfulfilled expectations is to ask myself if the unwanted behavior is life-threatening or will seriously affect the child's future. In using the thinking solution I changed my question from "Why won't they do it?" to "What's really important?" I do require that my kids pick up their room once a week, but I can't get too excited over that being done imperfectly. I can get excited over driving drunk, dropping out of school, not using birth control, illicit drug use, and criminal behavior. Luckily for me, I have not had to deal with any of these problems in other than minute doses. My kids were pretty easy to raise when it came to the dangerous stuff. They all seemed to join me in the determination to stay alive and have choices about their future.

Pick your battles carefully and be aware of your thoughts (the thinking solution). Pondering why the child is acting a certain way can use up much of your valuable energy. You will, and probably should, require changes in behavior, but I would avoid expending much energy on "why." One of my children, when asked why she cut school, said, "It's more fun to be at the mall with my girlfriend than in class." Good reason! It probably is more fun to be at the mall, but still I required a change in behavior—staying at school.

The Art of Selecting Consequences

When you are using videotalk, you need to include something that motivates the child to comply with your request. Does she care about time on the phone? Does she care about having a friend overnight? Does he want to rent video games or movies? *Tie your request for action to what the child wants.* Some parents are concerned that this is "bribery," but if you look up the definition of bribery, you will find that the dictionary says giving someone something to "induce him to act dishonestly." Getting someone to clean his room, come in by curfew, do homework, and so forth is not acting dishonestly.

Lisa was a single mom. Her son's passion was video games; the third grade's teacher's passion was math. Lisa kept getting notes from the teacher about Nathan's incomplete math sheets. A conference led to the following plan: every day the teacher would send home a note telling Lisa whether that day's math sheets had been completed. If they were, then Nathan could play an hour of video games; if not, no video games that evening. Lisa was careful not to select any consequence that would be a problem for her. For example, she avoided prohibiting Nathan from being able to play outside with friends, because she got things done during that time. He could also still watch television, but Lisa knew that was not his biggest passion. Nathan did not become the best mathematician in the class, but he did get all his homework done, which satisfied both his mother and the teacher and led to significant improvement in his grades.

There are three guidelines for consequences I have set for myself and coach parents to set for themselves:

> Be sure that the consequence is not too much work for you.

Pick something that matters to the child.
Keep the big picture in mind.

Grounding for a short period of time may be tolerable for you, but think carefully before enforcing a two- or three-day grounding—*you* may feel like a P.O.W. by the end of it. You might consider taking television away for a night, particularly if you don't really approve of it, but if missing your favorite show becomes a casualty of your consequence, don't do it. Taking a phone out of a child's room is probably not too much work for you, but be sure that you don't end up standing guard over your phone for that period of time. Select consequences that have *your* comfort in mind. The thinking solution concept then is to ask, "What is not going to be too much work, fits with my values as a parent, and will still be a consequence to the child?"

Sometimes it can be worthwhile to strain yourself in making a consequence. My youngest child would feign illness to stay home from school. The first couple of times he stayed home claiming to be sick my pattern was to say that there would be no friends or television until after school was out for the day. That pattern was ineffective. The consequences escalated to making him stay in bed until school was over. Sitting in his room, keeping him in bed, came close to the limit, but it did get the results I wanted—no more fake illnesses. A day of confinement in bed with no television, for a normal active child who isn't sick, is a severe consequence and the problem was eliminated. If I had to do that repeatedly, I couldn't have done it.

The second guideline is to pick a consequence that matters to the child. Here you are using a thinking solution by asking, "What would matter enough to my child to get her to change?" I was having a conversation with my now adult daughter about consequences. She pointed out that I had enforced a consequence that utterly suited her rather than punished her: I made her go to her room for an hour. Since she was a self-contained, self-reliant child who loved being alone in her room, going to her room was no negative consequence at all! Somehow, *forbidding* her to go to her room never entered my mind as a satisfying consequence, but I could have thought of some task (such as mopping a floor), that would have benefited me and, at the same time, taken her away from her sanctuary.

Third, keep the big picture in mind. As a way of moderating the thinking solution of the last point (what matters to the child), you need to be careful not to remove things that are healthy building blocks in the child's self-esteem. A boy I was working with was not performing well in school. The parents knew that he loved Boy Scouts and they wanted to pull him out of Scouts as a punishment. I was against that move. If a child is not doing well in school, don't take away an activity he *is* doing well at, if you think it's a worthwhile activity. I wanted my children to have friends, so grounding as a consequence was rarely my first or even second choice. I also did not take away sports or music or clubs (Scouts) or anything that I thought ultimately contributed to a child's development. Video games, trips to the movies, desserts, candy, television—those were the options from which I selected a consequence.

Trust yourself as a parent. I have seen too many disasters where parents fell into a trap of assuming that only professionals were capable of making decisions about their child. In the worst case parents began to think that an institution was going to do better than they could to help the child. I have heard parents consider the option of a mental hospital more easily than I think they should. There are children who might benefit from inpatient care, but not those with your run-of-the-mill behavior problems. If you have a child who is hallucinating and thinks people are trying to poison him, then medications and a short stay in the hospital might help. I generally prefer the least invasive treatment: light on medications and heavy on creativity.

Getting Your Co-Parent to Parent

Unless you are a single parent, the solutions and consequences you choose to use with your children will be either opposed or supported by your co-parent. If you get support, there is no problem. But if your partner either goes off the deep end with consequences or does not enforce anything, then you've got a problem. Parents who balance each other well and agree on consequences are definitely on the rare side.

If you feel the other parent, stepparent, or parental figure is too harsh, you can help to agree to experiment with each other's strategy for a particular time period—for example, a month. (This is a form of compromise from the action solutions.) Assuming your co-parent is not abusing the child, you could agree to go with his rules for one month, if he will go with yours for the next month, to see which works best. In therapy I've found this method to be successful only about half the time, because usually, when parents get stuck on a discipline issue, it is their relationship that is the problem and not the difference in parenting values. If chafing over discipline escalates to a level where no week passes without a conflict over parenting, apply the strategies from this book to the relationship and parenting, take a parenting class together, or get therapy.

If a co-parent does not participate in consequence setting and enforcing, changing patterns and videotalk can be helpful in eliciting a response.

Leanne had tried lecturing Jim about what an absent father he was; she had also complained and shoved books about "better parenting" in his hands. Finally she decided to give up going for a big change and instead just pick one little thing she wanted Jim to do with the children when she was not there. She looked for one small change to help her feel less like a single parent. Using the principles of videotalk, she translated the vague term "better parent" into specific requests: "Jim supervising the children while they clean up the kitchen, so that the dirty dishes from the after-school snacks are in the washer, all food items

from the after-school snacks are in the washer, all food items are put away, and all globs of food are wiped off the kitchen table and kitchen counters." The kids would come home from school and make a mess having after-school snacks. She would come home to the duties of making dinner, but first have to clean up the kitchen to even get started. With such crystal-clear requests in hand, Jim was willing and able to do this, particularly since it took less than ten minutes. It was not a profound change, but it did help Leanne feel less alone as a parent and more listened to as a partner.

Dumping Maternal Guilt

Just as in marital relationships, most of the women I know take the lead in parenting. Unfortunately, the side effect of feeling responsible is to feel guilty about having to be away from the children. Guilt over working is something I, and all the working women I know, have struggled with. I would never say, "Don't work." My life would have been an absolute disaster without a job. I would not have had the same confidence to cope with parenting, and my children's security would have been disrupted, given the changes in my household. Not working was never an option for me, so, like nearly every woman I know, I felt bad about times away from my children and I kept my career somewhat in check in order to be available to them. As children they never complained about my working, and the adult children have never said anything that implied they felt bad about it. In fact, they've told me they felt proud of me and bragged about my accomplishments. In spite of all that, the boogieman of guilt was a familiar companion, lurking around the corner, ready to spring on me at any time.

Rituals of parenting and of career accomplishments helped move me through these feelings. Ceremonial mother events, such as the Mother's Day celebration at school, or rituals with my career, such as graduation, helped me define myself as firmly planted in both those roles. Taking time to participate in at-

rituals of connections with my children, such as a bedtime routine and waffles on Saturday mornings, helped me fend off my feelings of guilt.

Have you ever read or heard it said that the problem with our world today is that the dads don't stay at home half the time? No, you haven't. The assumption is that it should be the mother who sacrifices her career—if she can afford to. With my last child, his father and I created a way to share the first three years equally. His work was mostly out of town. I would structure my schedule to be home with our baby when his father was gone, and then he would take care of our son when he was back and I was seeing clients. After the first three years, the duties shifted more onto my shoulders, but the hardest part was over. I know other couples who have both gone to half-time jobs with the birth of a child and my hope is that this will be a trend.

The best way I know to deal with maternal guilt is to try to be with your child as much as you can, while still honoring your commitment to your career and yourself as a person. Whenever possible, pay someone else to do the tasks that take away from time with your child, like hiring a housekeeper to clean the house. Know that your values and your love, even if not available in person on a twenty-four-hour basis, are the guiding force in that child's life. Have fun and play in little ways, such as stopping for a moment of playful wrestling or a pillow fight while cleaning a room together.

I am now at the stage when my older children have become great sources of friendship and fun for me, and I think I am for them as well. Of course, we had to go through a time of separation from one another as they formed their own identities. But we weathered that phase. Now, my personal guideline for dealing with a child over eighteen is, "Never say anything to your adult child you would not say to a friend your own age." If you follow that guideline, then you can make an enjoyable transition from being a mom to being a friend with whom your grown child can be open.

Boomerangs! Coping with Grown Children

As economic challenges continue to confront our country, more mothers of grown children are dealing with the "boomerang generation"—launched children who return to live at home awhile. The best guidelines for the actions you request from adult children living in your home are the same actions you would expect and request from any adult roommate living in your house. Sometimes it is better for the adult-child if you hold him or her accountable for doing whatever is necessary to move towards self-support. You may be comfortable supporting grown children as long as they are attending school, but you have to look at your own individual circumstances. The most frustrating situation is the adult-child who has a baby whom you also wish to protect. Insisting a grown child leave home is one thing; sending a grandbaby out in the world is another.

Kathy's daughter, Erin, had a one-year-old daughter, Nicky, from a brief marriage. Erin, who was twenty years old, had not developed a career and Nicky's father did little to contribute to the child's care or support. Kathy could not bring herself to say, "Tough! You made your bed, now lie in it," mostly because of her concern for Nicky. Kathy let Erin move home and then they negotiated the rules at home and the rules about working. Kathy did require that Erin get a job and that she do most of Nicky's daily care. After a rough start, where Erin took advantage of the free baby-sitting for "partying," Kathy made it clear that she would sit for work or school-related activities but not for dating. Once they had worked out these details and Erin maintained her job, they found living together pretty comfortable for all of them. However, they also negotiated a goal for when Erin would move out and began a savings plan so that she would have sufficient funds to be independent.

I am mother of the four interesting children whom I have raised or am still raising. They have chosen fields that delight me and are each so unique. One is a successful rock musician, another is making a living as a writer, another is a jazz musician beginning college, and the third is a delightful little kid still in grade school. With them I have used the thinking solution to change from "why are they doing what they are doing" to "what" questions, focused on actions instead of their motives or labels, used my unconscious to "keep my cool," and rituals to keep my connection with them. I have been very fortunate to have children who did not ruin my theories!

I also feel very fortunate to have had the opportunity to have a job that I found so fascinating that I probably would have been willing to do it for free. The next chapter deals with the application of solutions to job challenges and career development.

PARENTING

Principles and Pathways

Trying too hard or giving up too soon ▪ As parents we sometimes work too hard to be sure everything is just right or we "throw in the towel" and give up on the child.
Are my expectations making both my child and me miserable? Is most of my time spent correcting my child? Have I given up on getting my child to change? Could I go for some small changes that might be in the right direction?

Rules and consequences ▪ Keep the rules few and simple and in videotalk. Focus on behaviors that will truly affect the child's future, such as drug usage, driving while intoxicated, dropping out of school.
Are my rules and the consequences I enforce making me miserable? Have I taken away something that contributed to my child's self-esteem, such as scouting or sports, instead of things that I know are not as valuable, such as cartoons and video games? Have I made so many rules that I am having to be a full-time cop? Could I simplify

my parenting by emphasizing what will keep my child healthy and alive and not destroy his or her future?

Getting a co-parent to participate ▪ Ask for what you want in videotalk. Change your pattern with the co-parent.

Have I asked in videotalk for exactly what I expect from my co-parent? Is there some way I could change my pattern with him?

Maternal Guilt ▪ Working outside the home is the only option for most women. Guilt can be dealt with partially through rituals of connection with the child.

Are there things you could hire out or assign that would leave you more free time if you are a mom employed outside the home? Do you have rituals that keep you connected to your child, such as cuddling at bedtime, meals together, special time on the weekends?

Limits on grown children who live in your home ▪ So many twenty-something children are returning home for financial reasons that it is necessary to set limits with them regarding expectations for work and activities around the home.

Have I made it clear to my adult children in my home what the videotalk version of my expectations are? Do I require job and/or school attendance? Have we set a goal for moving out?

Eight

Career

*L*AURA HAD BEEN ON an upper-level management track. She and Ted had been married for twelve years when the urge to have children overtook them. Ted had made partner in his law firm five years before and they were very secure financially. Kevin and Jessie were born two years apart and Laura struggled to find reliable child care for them. They had tried a live-in nanny; they tried day-care; but Kevin was three and Jessie was only one and Laura was constantly guilt-ridden. When she made the decision to take a year or two leave from her job, her boss expressed frustration and resentment that she put her children before "the team" they had built over the last five years.

At first Laura was in heaven staying home. She finally had time to enjoy the children, time to catch up on getting things organized, time to even squeeze in a nap. It was great—at first. Then Laura began to notice that, when she would meet someone for the first time, she would start defending herself when asked what she did. She found herself embarrassed about her homemaker-mom status.

She also felt frustrated about her body. She had not been able to lose the weight she had gained with two pregnancies and she found herself withdrawing sexually from Ted. She also felt that she had less and less interesting things to say to Ted and, anyway, he was tired and did not want to talk much after he came home. This lack of communication had not been a problem when she had spent the day at her office. More worrisome to her was that because of his job as a trial attorney, Ted would be out of town, sometimes for weeks at a time. She began to suspect he was having an affair. She was correct and when she confronted him, he asked for a divorce. Laura was suddenly in a huge financial bind, in addition to the emotional shock and trauma. They had created a luxurious lifestyle, but she had given up her job. It took six months for her to find a job at two-thirds the salary of her former position, plus she had to start from zero in accruing benefits.

"Why was I such a sucker?! Why didn't I insist that we *both* shift to part-time work? Why did I let myself be lulled into believing that our marriage would be forever, when I know nearly half of all marriages end in divorce?" Laura was almost as angry at herself for not taking greater precautions as she was with Ted for leaving.

Although the settlement and child support Laura received were generous, she knew that by giving up those two years, she had lost career ground that would take her twice as long to recover. It was wonderful that she had had that time with her young children, but the cost in self-esteem and the lack of long-term security for the children financially had been a big price.

Give Up the Ship—But Don't Give Up Your Job

Laura made a mistake that many women make: she relinquished the security blanket of her career. Another woman I know had been a licensed practical nurse. After she married, she became a homemaker. Her husband said, "It's been three years since you worked. Let's stop paying this $20 a year for your LPN license." She agreed. When her husband was unexpectedly laid off from his job, she found out that she would have to take a $500 course to reinstate her license!

When women have jobs and careers, potential disasters such as a divorce or the death of a spouse are not nearly as devastating. It isn't even just the money. The validation of being appreciated for the work you do, no matter what that work is, helps you keep on an even keel when relationship or parenting crises rock your boat. For me, work was a life-saver. If I had not had my career when I faced divorce, it would have been ten times harder. Work is social relationships; work is the way you structure your life. My first and foremost message to you is work or prepare to work, now!

Work and the money it earns translate into power either in a relationship or on your own. I know a therapist who will not do marital therapy unless the woman has some means of supporting herself. The therapist feels that the power issues in the marriage cannot be resolved as long as one person is financially dependent on another. Of course, this is one of those beliefs to be wary of I mentioned in the thinking solution. I do not assume every couple has a power issue; however, many couples do have power issues and inability to earn money can tip the scales still further.

Just as important as making money is learning what to do with it after you've made it. I have read and re-read Jane Bryant Quinn's *Making the Most of Your Money*. It is a comprehensive guide to managing your money that I think women, especially, should read.

It may sound like I think being a homemaker is a bad decision. I was a homemaker for seven years and I thoroughly enjoyed it. It is a valid and satisfying choice, but a risky one. Later in my life I realized that I would have been much more financially secure and my children's college education accounted for, if I had worked sooner and been in charge of the money. With both my husbands, I tended to abdicate my money-managing abilities, unconsciously falling prey to the cultural assumption that certain genitalia determine competence in financial matters. That was a mistake!

If you choose to be a homemaker, at least use some of that wonderful time to get prepared—just in case. What made it more fun for me to stay home with my kids was that I began to nibble away at a master's degree while I was baking bread, making yogurt, and sewing drapes for the family room. If you are going to stay home, do something that might lead to future employment, should the necessity to work arise. Even a part-time job is some security. Having to put on your resume that you have not had any employment for fifteen years is a big disadvantage, unless you earned a degree, mastered computer skills, or acquired some other skill that would be appreciated by an employer.

Many women choose to work for their husbands' businesses or practices. While that is not the worst idea, the outside validation is not available in those "in-house" circumstances and, should he have a mid-life crisis and decide he needs to be free, where would that leave you? Get, and keep, an independent means of your own security. I know I may sound a little preachy, but I have worked with so many women who have had the devastation of a divorce or death of a spouse made so much worse by not having a way to support themselves and being emotionally isolated. I feel I would be shirking my job of helping women if I did not address this issue.

Applying the Dreaming Solution

Getting a career started, asking for a raise, taking on tough projects all require your ability to daydream success. If you cannot imagine it, it will be very difficult, if not impossible, to achieve it. And if you're so nervous in the actual situation that you tremble, shake, and stutter, you will also have trouble achieving it. Enter imagery and relaxation, two very crucial inner tools. I have had to fire a few people in my day and imagery helped me be able to breathe and think clearly through those ordeals.

Karen had been laid off by the phone company. She had started working for them twenty-two years ago and could not imagine what she might do now. Because she had accumulated so many years of service, the severance package was extensive enough that she could get by for a number of months—even years if she radically changed her lifestyle. We talked about her alternatives of returning to school or looking for another job. She decided that she wanted to get another job, but perhaps in a more "people-oriented" position. She had had experience in personnel and so she investigated getting into rehabilitation—but she was terrified of the prospect. To handle her fear, she applied the dreaming solution.

I suggested that she go to where she would make her job application, and, if she could do so discreetly, look at the waiting room, taking note of pictures on the wall, a clock, a calendar—anything that she might use as a signal to go into trance. She selected three locations where she wanted to apply and spied on the environments, picking objects she could use to focus upon while in the waiting room. She used one of my audiotapes on self-hypnosis to practice relaxation and imagined the object she selected in the waiting room as the signal to relax. Then she imagined an extensive and successful interview, in which she even joked a little with the interviewer. This preparation gave her the courage to schedule the actual interviews. She was interviewed by two of the agencies she had selected and hired by one of them.

Applying the Feeling Solution

Sometimes what it takes to move your career along is to lose your job. I know that sounds contradictory, but I have met many women who started their own businesses because they lost the security they had in a corporate job. Of course, the first step is to get over the loss of the job. It can often feel so personal and devastating, particularly in a small company, that you may need to do a ritual to acknowledge and dissolve lingering negative feelings.

A woman called my talk show saying that she had not worked in two years because she was so hurt in her last position. Office politics had left her feeling so betrayed, both personally and professionally, that she had been unwilling to risk getting into a job again. We talked about what had actually happened, and I pointed out that she had learned some important lessons about unwise self-disclosure with co-workers and about keeping out of office politics as much as possible. Then we planned a ceremony to symbolize her letting go of the past. She was to write a letter to her boss and the friends who betrayed her at work and then bury the letters in the woods where she liked to walk. I later received a note from her telling me that she was applying for jobs again and that the ritual had been a turning point for her.

Applying the Thinking Solution

Losing a job can be an opportunity to become a hero in your own life. Like our last example, the woman learned some valuable lessons that she could take with her. She became a hero through conquering her fears and applying for jobs again. Heroes may win battles, but sometimes those battles are ones we never see from the outside. Losing job security and the threat of financial difficulties can act as a catalyst to explore what your personal assets are and what you truly want to do. My personal guideline is to find a job that you love so much that you would be willing to do it for free (if you could afford to!).

Meg had been a psychotherapist for sixteen years. The hospital she worked for was laying off people and her job was one of those eliminated. She took the opportunity to reconsider what she truly wanted to do. She was definitely tired of working in an environment of chronic mental illness. She also knew that, with the changes in reimbursement from managed-care companies, this was a terrible time to try to set up a private practice. Initially she was stuck in a thinking problem of "Why is this happening to me?" But, as I talked with her over lunch, she moved into "How could this be an opportunity for me?" Being laid off was her opportunity to change fields.

She had an undergraduate degree in education and a master's

in counseling. She thought she might like to teach. She had done only her student teaching and had little experience, but the hours, summers off, and working with children appealed to her. With great enthusiasm she updated her training and then entered the job market as an elementary teacher. The first year she could find only substitute jobs. Since substitute teachers are often the victims of students, those jobs gave her the chance to practice her dreaming solution of staying relaxed no matter what was happening around her. The best news about the substitute work was that it gave her the opportunity to make lots of contacts in schools. Ultimately she landed a full-time job, which she loves to this day. As Meg looked back over her life, this sequence had been perfect for her. Now that she was in her late thirties and had had children, she appreciated the school children in a way she never could have, had she started her teaching career in her twenties. She took a situation that was a disappointment and ultimately convinced herself it was perfect for her. She applied a thinking solution by changing her view of a situation from one of failure to one of success and used actions all along the way to create a good outcome.

There are many practical ideas that my friends, callers, and clients have used in finding their way into the workplace. Network with anyone who knows you are, or could be, a productive and reliable worker, even if you have done only volunteer work so far. Networking could mean eating lunch with or calling an old boss or co-worker on the phone, sending a letter to someone who knows the market and your abilities, or asking someone to speak to someone else on your behalf. Someone will have seen your potential and your skills. Get your foot in the door, even if it isn't your dream job, particularly if the job offers advancement opportunities and experience. Think of something you could suggest that would mark you as a creative person who has unique talents to offer. Have your resume delivered by courier, if you can afford it. Send the company a "thank you" note for the interview. As we talked about in discussing the actions solutions, observe and ask friends how they got the job they have and use their ideas. All these actions might help.

Multiple Fishing Lines

In addition to keeping your finger in the job market even if you are a full-time homemaker, I also want to suggest that you cross-train. I have been cross-training for alternative jobs for the past five years, even though I did not start out thinking, *It's time to cross-train now.* I think of it as having four fishing lines in the water to see which line gets a bite. The first and foremost line is working as a therapist, at which I have proved my competence and which I will probably always do, to some degree. The second is the writing line; I have been writing books for the past nine years and I may very well devote most of the rest of my life to that. The third line is training other therapists. I have taught therapists all over the United States and in New Zealand and Europe. I will probably keep doing that a bit, although the travel is not appealing. The last is the media line. I have enjoyed doing a radio talk show and am making efforts to explore other possibilities in that area.

Every woman could benefit from having a second possibility of a career, just as a good safety net. Learning extra skills, cross-training for other jobs, staying open to new opportunities and possibilities are all ways you can secure your future and be ready for changes, which seem inevitable.

Problems on the Job

Problems commonly faced by women in the workplace include: dealing with critical or unpredictable bosses, sexual harassment, job upheavals caused by downsizing, and subtle, undermining, gender-related assumptions (such as a woman can't handle the really tough tasks).

So far the women I have mentioned have used the feeling solution (rituals), the dreaming solution (imagery), and the thinking solution (mythologizing their lives). Action solutions (action requests) are also a staple of surviving in the day-to-day world of work.

Action Solutions to Criticism

Candace was in trouble at work. Her boss, Emily, complained that Candace was "not responsible enough." Candace was afraid she was about to get sacked, so she came to see me. I explained the concept of videotalk: asking Emily to be specific about exactly what types of behaviors looked like and sounded like *responsibility* to her and what did not look and sound like responsibility. Emily had no trouble getting specific: being on time was responsible; getting reports ready on time was responsible; doing follow-up calls with customers and keeping her informed about Candace's activities with customers. was responsible. *Now* Candace finally had some ideas about the priorities. She was able to make a sustained effort; four months later Emily commented on Candace's turnaround. I wonder if Emily learned more about getting specific from that experience as well.

Action Solutions to Sexual Harassment

When sexual harassment first became a publicized issue, it occurred to me that many of the common concerns in this area could be helped by videotalk. I remember noticing that people I worked with were reluctant to joke around with me in the usual way. I even found myself a little leery about things I used to say, now wondering if my comments might be misconstrued. At my counseling center we used videotalk to identify exactly what kind of behavior constituted sexual harassment and then we were able to resume our old ways of joking and kidding. Although the definition of sexual harassment included "unwanted sexual comments or contact," we agreed that tossing around innuendoes in a room with twelve staff members during a meeting was not a problem—for us.

Harvey was a fifty-five-year-old counselor at a place where I supervised the therapy. In a staff meeting he kept referring to his female clients as "girls." We assumed he was talking about women under twenty-one years of age. When we found out he was talking about a woman in her thirties as a "girl," I asked Harvey that he not used that term to describe a grown woman. I told him that for me "girls" was videotalk of "subtle put-downs" of women. Harvey made excuses for himself because of his age, but, after an apology, he did stop referring to grown women as girls.

Videotalk, unfortunately, is only going to handle well-intentioned guys, like Harvey, who goof up. Serious offenders, however, are not making inadvertent errors but deliberately trying to intimidate and control women. If you need information on what to do about sexual harassment, try the handy book, *The 9 to 5 Guide to Combating Sexual Harassment* by Ellen Bravo and Ellen Cassedy. It is a practical, solution-oriented book that outlines what steps to take, from clearly saying "no" all the way to legal actions.

Action Solutions to Gender-Related Assumptions

Usually more subtle than sexual harassment but potentially as harmful are gender-related assumptions that are made about your priorities as a woman.

Debra assumed that she would be the likely candidate for the position of managing the East Coast division of her company. She would be competing with another person—a man—for the position, but from her perspective the choice seemed clear: she had three more years of experience and more education than her competitor. When she did not receive the management position, she talked to her boss, who had decided her fate. He did not come out and say, "It's because you're a mother," not being into lawyers, but he indirectly communicated that message by saying, "Why are you so disappointed? The job would have meant traveling at least twice a month. That's no fun." Though Debra would never have sued her boss for this flimsy rationalization, it was clear to her that he had erroneously assumed that she would be less willing to fulfill the position's requirements because she was a mother. (He could have *asked* her at least.) The man who did receive the job was a father of two preschool-aged children, but that same assumption was not made about him. Debra did ask that the next time a promotion that might involve travel was available, her boss put aside his ideas that she might not want to travel and support her for the promotion. (This was videotalk for, "Don't be biased against me because I am a woman.")

Even though there are subtle and not-so-subtle biases against women in the marketplace, I feel hopeful about the future of women. The fact that in recent years more women than men have graduated from college and gotten graduate degrees suggests that there will be a time when the majority gender (women) will finally occupy the leadership positions that they deserve. It will probably not happen in our lifetime, but it *will* happen. In this era, it may be that the main way women can create successful and powerful job experiences is by starting their own businesses, as I did. The changes for women seem slow to me, but then, I always want everything "fixed" as quickly as it can be!

CAREER
Principles and Pathways

Jobs are a source of satisfaction and security ▪ When women face personal crises a job, with its satisfactions and the financial security it offers, can be part of the recovery for herself and her children.
Are you prepared to support yourself should you need to? Do you have

the training and experience to get a job or change jobs if it becomes necessary? Is there anything you have to do to secure your future?

The dreaming solutions help you imagine and attain success ▪ By imagining success and managing your anxiety you can create changes in your career or take the steps necessary to have a career.

Do you need to use relaxation and self-hypnosis to be able to achieve your next career goal (such as applying for a position)? Do you need to manage your anxiety to expand what you do in your career?

The feeling solutions help you leave job disappointments behind ▪ By using rituals to get over past disappointments in your career, you free yourself to move forward.

Are there upsetting things that have happened to you in your career that block your progress now? Could you design a ceremony to get over these past disappointments?

The thinking solution helps you ask the right questions about your career ▪ If your career has taken a discouraging turn, instead of asking why things have turned out the way they have, ask what you need to do next to create success.

Are there ways that you talk about your career that keep you from moving forward? Do you need to change the questions that you ask yourself about your career?

Action solutions to problems women face in the workplace include videotalk ▪ When you encounter criticism or sexism in the workplace, videotalk can help you clear up the difficulty.

Are you given feedback about your work that is too general to respond to? Could you ask for a videotalk description of what your boss, employee, or co-worker would like from you? If some remark is made that you feel has sexist overtones, could you make an action request that those kinds of remarks not be made in the future?

Nine

Violence and Violations

J ENNY WAS A DELIGHTFUL, beautiful young woman
in her mid-twenties who had moved to Omaha several years prior to the time I saw her. She had wanted to get
away from her hometown, which was in another state. I soon
learned why.

As a popular sixteen-year-old she dated one of the football
stars of her high school. One warm July evening, when she did
not have a date with John, she and her best friend Lisa had split
a six-pack of beer while sitting on a blanket by the creek outside
of town. They decided that burgers were the next needed addition to their small party, so they went to the local fast-food
restaurant. Jenny had consumed four of the six beers and was
not thinking straight. John, whom she'd been seeing for two
months arrived with three other guys—all local high school
football stars. They had been drinking, too. They said, "Hey,
Jenny, come for a ride with us."

Lisa had a premonition that this was not going to turn out
right. "Jenny, don't. I don't like the way they're acting. Something's not right," Lisa warned. Lisa went to the counter to
place their order. John, bolstered by the cheers of his team-
mates, grabbed Jenny and threw her over his shoulder and into
Brad's car. They took off with Jenny. Lisa returned to find
Jenny gone.

In the car Rick said, "My parents are out at the country club tonight for a party. Let's take her to my house."

Jenny heard them talking but it all seemed like a fog. She kept thinking about John, her boyfriend. After all, he had been a gentleman for the last two months. *He wouldn't let anything happen to me,* she thought. *They're just kidding. Nothing's going to happen.* She was wrong.

At Rick's house they forced Jenny into his bedroom, locked the door, and raped her; a couple of the guys participated together, but mostly they raped her one at a time. She was terrified, but at the same time, it just seemed too horrible to be happening. Panic and unreality competed in her mind. When the boys had finally spent themselves, they left her alone in the bedroom. Jenny crawled into a closet and hid, clutching her torn clothes and trying to make herself into the tiniest ball possible.

Fortunately, Lisa had sobered up. It was like a dip in an icy shower to discover that Jenny had disappeared. Lisa enlisted a strongly-built male friend, Doug, to help her look for Jenny. They searched some of the "necking" places first, then the pond where lots of beer parties usually happened, and finally they went house to house of all the boys she had seen in the car. When they reached Rick's house, they saw Brad's car—the car that Jenny had left in. By this time, Rick's parents had come home. When Lisa and Doug pulled up, Rick saw them from his window and became concerned about his parents finding out what had gone on that night.

Lisa began to shout the moment Rick opened the front door. Rick tried to get Lisa to lower her voice. Lisa spat the words in Rick's face. "I don't give a damn what your parents think! I want to see Jenny and I want to see her now!" Rick, followed by Lisa and Doug, searched for Jenny and found her huddled in the closet of Rick's bedroom. Lisa threw a robe around Jenny and with an arm cradling Jenny's stooped shoulders guided her slowly to Doug's car. Jenny was in such pain, she was barely able to walk. Rick's parents emerged from their bedroom just as Lisa and Jenny were getting in the car.

Lisa delivered Jenny to her shocked parents. They all went to the hospital and began the frustrating, painful process of charging the boys with rape.

None of the boys, who were the children of prominent citizens, served even one night in jail. They were released with a "slap on the hand" for repeatedly raping Jenny. The town, and particularly the high school, seemed to blame Jenny. She was ostracized by many students who formerly had been her friends. The school administrators made certain that she did not share classes with her attackers the first semester while the trial was happening. But by the second semester, they apparently believed she should have adjusted or "gotten over it" and were unwilling to alter her schedule. Being in the same building with the rapists and seeing them in the hallways at school led to flashbacks of that torturous summer night. Being in the same room with them was more terrifying than she could endure. She had to transfer to a different school to finish her high-school education.

Jenny came to see me because, although her life was proceeding well—she had married a good man, was finishing her bachelor's degree, and had a one-year-old son—recently she had experienced a recurrence of the flashbacks. She had returned to her hometown to attend the wedding of a former classmate and at the wedding she had seen one of her attackers. She had read my book on self-hypnosis and wanted just one hypnosis session to help her get back on track (the dreaming solution). The one session seemed to catalyze a real breakthrough for her. She wrote, telling me that she had stopped having the flashbacks and, in spite of the number of years that had passed, she had written to the school administrators to tell them how unfair and insensitive it was to expect her to casually share classes with her rapists (an action solution, which also had a quality of a ritual from the feeling solution category).

Problems of violence and violations fall into three groups: rape in adulthood, sexual abuse during childhood, and domestic violence. Domestic violence is so common and so disturbing, I have devoted a separate chapter to it. Furthermore, because rape and sexual abuse have usually been in the past, while domestic violence may be ongoing, the solutions and healing processes differ.

When I met Jenny I thought of my own history as a teenager. I had partied as a kid. What had happened to Jenny could have happened to me. I know that one in eight women is raped sometime during her life. Our country is dangerous for women. *Women* have to be on guard for their safety even though rape is a problem to which both men and women in our culture need to respond.

Thankfully, I was never attacked by a stranger, but I did have a frightening experience in which I felt forced to have sex. A man I had been in a relationship with for some time had been out with the guys and came home drunk. It was late, but we started to make love. I began to feel that something was different. The message became clear, not from words, but from the way I was being restrained, that it would take a real battle on my part to stop him at this point. If I had any choice there, I certainly didn't experience it. Did I press charges? No way! I was too embarrassed. If I had said to him that I thought he had raped me, he would have thought I had slipped a cog. I did make it clear that I would never have sex with him again if he had been drinking, and I kept that commitment. Although the incident was never repeated, the relationship suffered permanent damage.

I have had many rape victims as clients and even more women (and some men) who were sexually abused as children. The statistics on women who have been sexually abused indicate that somewhere between 30 and 50 percent of women have been victims of sexual abuse. If you tend to doubt statistics and their makers, even cutting those numbers in half represents a national shame and disgrace.

Healing Actions

If any kind of violation has happened to you, how can you best apply the solution-oriented approach? In counseling women who have been violated in the past, I have observed that acknowledging the violation is the first step (the feeling solution). Whenever possible in terms of logistical and emotional concerns, holding the perpetrator accountable for the violation is the second step. The third step is reclaiming those aspects of the self that may have been temporarily expunged by the violation, such as the sense of *owning* one's own body, the ability to express anger, and natural access to sexual feelings. The loss of these freedoms keeps the violation alive for women abused as children. The final step can be the creation of a ritual to symbolize healing of the ongoing sense of violation.

Acknowledging the Violation

The first step of acknowledgment can be very difficult; some women are ashamed to admit that they were abused. The oppression of shame is most intense when the perpetrator is a family member. I spent six sessions working with one woman before she could tell me what had happened to her. Verbalizing what happened makes the event seem so much more real— which is why it can feel impossible to do. But having *done* it— finally telling someone—it then feels surprising to have *not* told someone for so long. You wonder how you have carried this burden. You can tell a therapist, a self-help group (in most communities the YWCA is a good resource), or even just write it down and have a friend read it. But somehow *you need to free yourself of this secret*. Secrecy sustains the sense of violation; self-disclosure cleanses it.

I know there are many women reading this book who have never told anyone about a date rape that happened to them, because they blamed themselves for getting into such a situation. Why? Because cultural and legal biases tell them so. Unfortunately, these biases against women victims infect us so much that we *ourselves* start believing that "we were asking for it." What I like to repeat to women who have been in this situation is, No matter what you wear or where you go, "yes" means *yes* and "no" means *no*. If you were too drunk or too scared to say no, that adds to the load of guilt. If that happened to you, I still want you to know that no one had the right to violate you, no matter what you had to drink, what you wore, where you were, or what bad choice in a date or ride home you might have made. If you believe that you caused this violation, *think again*. Develop another idea (thinking solution) about what kind of person would violate another human being.

Requesting Accountability

If it is possible, hold the perpetrator accountable. I know that horror stories abound about women who pressed charges, only to have themselves be made to look like fools by defense attorneys. At least go to the hospital and preserve evidence if this happens to you or a friend. You can always drop the charges, but you need to give yourself the option of reaching for justice later. In the action solution, you take action first and feelings follow. If you take the action of defending yourself through legal channels, then you may feel more empowered and less intimidated.

Single and in her mid-thirties, Alice was a lonely woman. She had had only two relationships that had lasted more than a year.

One day, she went to her market, which had a deli section where customers eat. As Alice was munching on her sandwich, a handsome man who was with a male friend at a nearby table, began to flirt with her. When she got up to do her shopping, he followed her around the store. It was summer, and at the fruit and vegetable aisle, he asked her if she would let him buy some cantaloupe and ice cream and then go to a park to have a picnic with him. She was hesitant but agreed.

At the end of their picnic, as she prepared to leave, he was a little pushy about kissing, but did not try much more than that.

However, for the next three months, he put on the big rush. He called her at least three times a day; he left a rose on her car; he sent her cute cards. She had never been treated so romantically. When I heard this story I thought, *I wish my husband would do things like that*. Then six months into the relationship she found out that he was married. She was not willing to give up on him though and asked him to leave his wife.

As Alice pressured him to get a divorce, their relationship became more and more conflictual. One evening he came over and "just seemed weird." He was disheveled; he seemed distracted and hostile. That night he raped her anally with a vibrator. She was a nurse and had the good sense to go to the hospital immediately and have the evidence collected (documentation of anal and other internal damages) so that she could press charges. He plea-bargained and he never served even one night in jail, but at least now he has a record.

He called and threatened her for pressing charges and Alice lived in fear for a long time. For more than a year, with the drawn-out trial and the fear that he would return, Alice never felt safe. Nevertheless, she had the courage to stick to her insistence that he be held accountable for his actions. Alice was a solution-oriented person. She joined the YWCA group for rape victims, educated her family about what she was going through in terms of the typical stages of recovery, did rituals to aid in her own healing, and worked on the explanations she told herself about the rape and the relationship. Letting go was made all the harder because she still loved him and she had had so little romantic love in her life. Eventually, however, she did heal and recover.

Reclaiming Your Self

Often when the violation occurred during childhood, the child splits off parts of her body or her feelings: her anger, because it is not safe to be angry; her body, which seems to be the cause of the horror; and her sexuality, the experience of which would only prove her perversity.

Debbie had been sexually abused by her mother's boyfriend for two years as a child. Now, as a grown woman, she was incapable of expressing anger. Her mother had not believed Debbie when she finally told her what was going on; in fact, Debbie had not been allowed to express *anything* negative about her experiences as a child.

As Debbie talked about these painful times of invasion and betrayal, she smiled. It was strange to listen to her talk about her secret horror with a smile on her face (although that kind of disparity between the *telling* of a trauma and the *feeling* of the trauma is something I have noticed with many victims of abuse).

Debbie designed a ritual that included writing to her mother, confronting her again about the violation. Her mother apologized, but it felt insincere and only marginally satisfying to Debbie. Then she wrote a letter expressing her rage to the perpetrator. Since she had no idea where he lived, she could only use this exercise as a ritual. She burned the letter along with a picture she drew of him.

In the months that followed the ritual, she began to express anger, if only tentatively at first. She experimented with me. When I did not abandon her when she was angry, she began to feel increasingly comfortable with her anger. She was then able to confront her mother with her anger in person, which seemed to complete the healing for Debbie.

Action Solutions to the Legacy of Violation

With women who have been abused, I ask the question, "How is this past trauma a problem for you now?" That way we get to an action solution—that is, what actions are happening now that need to stop happening, or what actions are not happening that need to happen.

Rachel had been raped four years ago by a boyfriend. He had expected the relationship to continue after the rape and he pursued her. She was twenty-four and had completely stopped dating after this event. She came to therapy because she knew she would eventually want to have a life that included a man and children. The videotalk answer to the question about how this is a problem now included getting over her phobia of men by making eye contact with men, speaking to men, and going on a date.

I asked Rachel to daydream about what she would be doing if she were beginning to get over being afraid of all men (dreaming solution). She said that she would start going to the singles group activities at her church; she would make eye contact with the men in her office; and she would start wearing something besides oversized clothes. She agreed to try those actions between sessions, which helped her move towards her goal of being less afraid of men.

The next hurdle came when she had agreed to go on her first date (action solution). Through self-hypnosis and relaxation activities (dreaming solution) and careful management of what she said to herself (thinking solution), she was able to not faint, vomit on, or run away from the very nice young man who had asked her out! She was still dating him the last time I saw her. Rachel had made use of the dreaming solution to learn to relax, the thinking solution to change her negative self-talk, and the action solution of accepting a date.

Judy was one of my more creative clients. She had already been in therapy, but after reading my book, *Making Friends With Your Unconscious Mind,* she felt that there was another method she wanted to explore in her attempts to heal the violation she had suffered.

Judy's father had sexually abused her by forcing her to have intercourse during all four years of high school. Her mother, at first, had not believed her, but even when she eventually did believe her, she took no action to stop her husband. To Judy, her mom seemed dead emotionally.

I asked her how she felt about confronting her father, but he had died, so she could only confront him symbolically. We considered various action options: letter writing, picture burning, or creating a clay statue to represent the experience. Ultimately she decided that the only action that would feel satisfying to her would be one that somehow broadcast the violation to her small town in Iowa. She decided to use defoliant (grass and weed killer) to write *child abuser* on the grave of her father. This small act of vandalism was deeply satisfying to her and she knew that next year the grass would grow back and the vandalism would repair itself.

Typical therapy in the field of sexual abuse places great emphasis on discussing the "typical phases" that abuse victims go through. I tend to stay away from that line of thinking except for emphasis on validating the woman's experience. As I pointed out in chapter 2 on the thinking solution, naming something tends to give it power and to even create something that might not have been there otherwise. You feel what you feel, and you may or may not fit perfectly into any categories. Experiment with what helps you feel the most healed and what lets you move on to the next phase in your life.

All these ideas and stories are from women who were abused in the past. Tragically, many women are in ongoing abusive and dangerous relationships in their current lives. The next chapter explores how to use the solution-oriented approach to escape from danger and abuse in a present relationship.

SOLUTIONS FOR VIOLENCE AND VIOLATION
Pathways and Principles

Acknowledge the violation ▪ Using the feeling solution of acknowledging both the events and your reactions to them is the first step in healing.
Have you been able to tell someone about a violation? If not, could you find someone whom you trust to tell of your experience?

Hold the perpetrator accountable ▪ If possible hold the perpetrator accountable by pressing charges or confronting him face to face. If that is not possible, create a ritual that confronts the perpetrator.
Are there any legal steps open to you? How would you like to confront the perpetrator? Is there a way to make that happen?

Reclaim yourself ▪ When violations occur, the victim tends to disown parts of herself (sexuality, anger, experiencing of the body). Part of the healing process is to reclaim the disowned part.
Is there some part of you that you have disowned as part of the violation process? Do you need to acknowledge that or take actions which would be the opposite of that disowning experience (caring for your body, having sex in a loving context, etc.)?

Rituals allow leaving trauma behind ▪ If you have suffered a violation, create a ritual that will symbolize that event and the leaving of that event in the past.
Is there a ritual you need to create to symbolize a violation? What would be the most appropriate symbol for you? What would be the best way to dispose of that symbol to represent your leaving it in the past?

Ten

Dangerous Relationships

"*P*AT, COULD YOU come over?"

"Jean, are you sick? What's wrong? You sound awful!"

"It's Evan. He beat me."

"Did you call the police? Where are the boys? Have you seen a doctor?" I panicked and overwhelmed her with a barrage of questions.

"Evan's mother was here. She did nothing to stop him nor did she call the cops. The boys were here, too. He blew up about his briefcase being left outside in the car, or some such stupid thing, and started beating me. The kids even had friends over. They were terrified and hid in their closets until it was all over. When I escaped long enough to punch in 911, Evan grabbed his keys and ran out of the house. An ambulance came and a paramedic checked me out. I wouldn't go to the hospital. There is a warrant out for Evan's arrest. He won't come back now."

"You know you have to divorce him. You can't live like this anymore."

"I will, Pat, I promise. Could you just come over? I need to see someone who cares and someone I trust."

On the way over to Jean's I tried to think of what I could bring to comfort her. I stopped and bought an ice pack. It was the first thing that came to mind, probably because a couple of weeks before I had managed to catch my size nine-and-a-half running shoes in the garden hose while moving the sprinkler, tripped, and bruised my knee and elbow. I love ice packs. I also thought flowers might cheer her up. As I was standing in line to pay for the flowers, I grabbed a couple packs of bubble gum for the boys. It must be living hell to see your mom beaten by your father.

In Jean's driveway I saw Jeff, her ten-year-old son. He looked like someone had punched him in the gut. He gave a lame "Thanks," to the bubble gum. I think he was embarrassed to see me there. It meant I knew that his dad had done an awful thing to his mom.

When I saw the swollen blue face of my dear friend, I felt violent myself. I had the flashing thought of getting a gun and taking care of this problem myself. Actually, that thought is totally inconsistent with my values, but I felt so angry about the suffering I saw before me.

Jean described in detail being chased, cornered, and having her thick black hair ripped out by his yanking, rage-filled hands. There were pieces of broken furniture stacked against the wall. I knew Jean couldn't stand a mess, even under these circumstances.

"On Monday, I'll get a restraining order against Evan for me and the kids and then I'll file for divorce."

"You can't stay here once the restraining order is served. He'll come and get you and the kids. You have to stay with me. Patrick [my nine-year-old] will think of it as a slumber party."

"Are you sure?"

"Jean, I want to get some sleep next week. If you're in my house with my security system protecting you, I'll sleep. If you're here, I won't."

We sat in silence while I tried to think of other things that would make her feel more safe. On some level, I wondered if it would ever be over. She had divorced him once already! He had gone through the abusers group at the Y. Evan claimed convincingly to have changed and Jean had married him again.

If needed, I would accompany her into divorce court myself and make sure she stuck with it this time.

I was afraid to ask the next question that was on my mind, because I didn't want to blame her. "Did you hit him or fight back?"

"No, Pat. Do you remember that I told you he nearly killed me the first time I was married to him. The last time I fought back, he stabbed me. He spent six months in jail for that. I never fought back again."

We sat there in her living room. It was utterly quiet, except for the ticking of an antique clock. I had a scary, Steven-King-movie feeling, but I dismissed it as a premonition and attributed it to the evil that had already happened in this house.

A month or two later, the boys were questioned again by the police in preparation for the court case against Evan. Jean was horrified at the details they remembered—including days of finding hunks of her hair all over the house. Those memories will probably never be completely erased, no matter how much time passes.

It has been four years since all this happened. Evan continued to visit the kids and intimidate Jean until he was forced to relinquish parental rights or face a judge for child abuse after punching the younger boy, Drew. He continues to phone, particularly around anniversaries of their marriage, the last beating, and the divorce. He uses the excuse of talking to the boys, but he often tries to get Jean engaged in what could become an argument.

Just yesterday Jean called me, irritated that Evan had sent a fax to her complaining about the dental bills for the boys. When she had spell-checked her reply to Evan on the office computer, she found that his name wasn't in the computer's dictionary. It offered the word *Evil* as a suggested alternative. We had quite a chuckle over that!

Although years have passed, I still worry about Jean. I fear that Evan might still kill her. But for now, she is alive and thriving. I count on her to continue to do so. We both know that it will take years for her to feel safe and healed.

Keys to Escape and Safety

Going through this with Jean was one of the more intense learning experiences of my life. I learned that strong, competent women tolerate this kind of danger and abuse much longer than you would ever expect. No training workshops, no amount of working with clients, quite prepared me for the emotional upheaval of dealing with a threatened and injured friend. I learned that friends or family members can be one of the keys to not being killed by an abusive spouse, and having a place to hide is crucial to escape. Shelters help with this, of course, but the attic guest rooms of friends aren't half-bad either. Money is also one of the keys to escape. Jean had just gotten a raise and she finally knew that she could make ends meet without being dependent on her abusive husband.

Jean used the best solution for dealing with violent relationships—she got out. But I know, from the statistics on women who are abused, that a majority will stay in the abusive relationship. If you can't leave, for whatever reason, and if no friend is hiding you in her house as you are reading this, don't despair. There *are* solutions you can still use.

If You Feel You Can't Leave . . .

The practical ideas of making enough money to support yourself and having an escape plan are part of utilizing the action solution. In violent families, learning to recognize and change patterns is crucial (the action solution). In almost all abusive relationships, both partners can tell you the exact signals forewarning escalation to violence.

Jeri had realized that Bill would sit on the couch with his arms folded across his chest, his legs extended and crossed at the ankles, before he would "blow up." Her usual pattern was to begin to sneak around the house like a whipped dog, dodging Bill. This only provoked him further, heightening the likelihood of violent outbursts. So she made plans to change her actions whenever that warning position was assumed. In essence, she developed her own safety plan. When she saw him sitting on the couch in this way, she would leave the house for at least an hour. Another plan: If any close friends or family members called, she had prearranged code words that would let them know this would be a good time to visit her. She kept a bag packed and hidden with a little money in it so that she could escape with the kids to her sister's house, if needed. When she changed her way of responding to Bill, *his* response of violence decreased significantly.

One typical pattern that occurs in violent relationships is that the abuser attempts to isolate the victim by cutting her off from family, friends, and work.

I met Joanne and Michael in premarital therapy. Michael had been married twice before, and after attending a relationship class that I had taught, he wanted to make sure he and Joanne were on the right track. I was touched by his concern, his romanticism, and his ability to be vulnerable with Joanne.

Five years later they returned: Michael had beaten Joanne while she was pregnant with their first child. First, he had succeeded in isolating her from her family, and because he was wealthy, he had convinced her to quit her job. Essentially she had no life outside their marriage. I encouraged Joanne to tell her sister about the violence and to return to her job, at least part-time.

After changing the isolation, the next thing needed was to identify and change patterns associated with the violence itself (which usually involved Joanne's withdrawing when Michael started to escalate). Michael agreed to leave the house for thirty minutes when the conflicts began to escalate.

Joanne used the thinking solution to change her part of the relationship. She used to try to understand *why* Michael was doing what he was doing; now she began to think about *what* she would do about the situation in terms of consequences, if he hit her again. She agreed to press charges if there was ever any more violence. I did not push Joanne to leave him, because I thought that he might possibly change, since he eagerly and voluntarily went to the abusers' group at the Y, and he did not claim that she had "made me do it," as so many of my clients had. Last time I heard from them, they were still together. I always have some fears in this area, because it is the most difficult challenge to change permanently, but people have to decide their own paths.

Women Abusers

One pattern I have noticed on occasion is that the woman strikes the first blow. As Carol Tavris pointed out in her book, *Anger: The Misunderstood Emotion,* 12 percent of men are violent in the home and about 12 percent of women are also violent in the home. The difference is that, given their greater strength together with comfort with weapons, men are much more deadly and destructive when violent. If you are the hitter, slapper, puncher, or kicker, how can you get yourself to stop?

Paula admitted that she had a dreadful temper and that she felt out of control often. Jerry had just about had it with her violence and the broken items in the house. Paula wanted to learn to be less reactive. We talked about patterns, and that seemed to help, but what turned Paula around the most was learning self-hypnosis. In trance she gave herself suggestions that whenever she saw Jerry, heard his voice, or even thought of him, that would be the signal for her to relax and breathe deeply, allowing all her problem-solving resources to come forward into her conscious thinking. For the first month she had to practice self-hypnosis daily, but gradually the new pattern of responding became automatic for her. "I had felt that I had no control over my reactions—but, now, Jerry couldn't upset me even if he tried."

Help a Friend or Family Member

Changing patterns, making consequences, using the thinking solution, and mastering self-hypnosis are all solutions that can lead to freedom from a violent relationship.

It may be that as you read this chapter a friend or relative who is in a violent relationship comes to mind. If you do have such a friend, know that there may be a few false starts before she actually has the courage to leave. Keep the number of a shelter for abused women handy for her. Offer to help her in any way you can. If she needs to be hidden for a while, arrange that for her, if you can. Find out about a local Y group, help your friend by offering to baby-sit the night she has to go to the group. (Baby-sit in *your* home, though.) Let your friend know that you will be there for her no matter what she decides, but that you are deeply frightened that she could be killed.

When you don't know someone personally who admits to having suffered from violence, it is easy to minimize the whole issue of violence against women. One of the factors that has contributed to our willingness to minimize is that other information about women has been exaggerated. In *Who Stole Feminism,* Christina Hoff Sommers pointed out that statistics about women have been misquoted and widely circulated. I agree that it can happen, as it did when figures about the number of women who have died from anorexia were circulated. The claim was made that about 150,000 women die each year from anorexia, when careful investigation reveals that the number is around 100 or less most years. What I do with all statistics that I hear about women is to check my own experience. How many women have I personally known who died of anorexia? None. I've known plenty who had bulimia and some who had anorexia, but no one I know had ever died of these problems.

When it comes to violent marital relationships, I have known plenty of women who have experienced violence. Out of the forty women who have worked for me over the last twenty years at my counseling center, I can name seven who were beaten by their spouses. Three of these were therapists. I personally observed bruises and blackened eyes on some of these women. Some told me about the nightmare marriages they had. One woman was married to a man who would sleep with a gun in the bed, threatening to kill her. When I checked my experience, it was clear to me that many women I have known and cared about have experienced violence at the hands of someone they loved.

You may be wondering if *you* are a victim of domestic violence. My personal standard is that any touching in anger—be it a push with an index finger in the chest, a shove, or a fist in the face—is violent and should not be tolerated. If at this point you have only had a shove, get help now. Do not take a chance on this pattern escalating. If only one woman who reads this chapter takes the actions necessary to make herself safe, then my life has been worthwhile.

SOLUTIONS FOR DANGEROUS RELATIONSHIPS
Principles and Pathways

Have a safety-escape plan ▪ If you are being abused, have a plan for getting away when it is necessary for your safety. Have a place to go, money and a bag hidden where you can get to it, and transportation.
If you are a victim of violence in the home: Do you know the number of a shelter or have a friend or relative to whose house you can go if you need to? Do you have some money hidden where you can get to it in an emergency? Have you agreed upon signals that you can give to a boss, friends, or relatives so that they know when you need help?

If you're staying, change patterns ▪ In most violent relationships there are patterns of escalation. Either you or the abusing spouse can change a part of the pattern.
Have you noticed the actions that usually precede the abuse? What could you do differently when you see those actions happening?

Be sure you are not the abuser ▪ In the home equal percentages of men and women are violent. Change your pattern if you are the abuser.

Have you been aware of what steps lead to your being violent? What could you do differently to change that pattern?

Help a friend who is being abused ▪ Offer shelter and support to a friend who is being abused. It may take her several tries to escape from the violent relationship.

Do you have a friend who is being abused? Does she know where to get help? Have you suggested a shelter or provided her with a place to escape to if needed?

Conclusion

I Can Only Tell You My Way

Women worldwide learn to doubt their views of reality, question their thinking, and mistrust their own judgments. I hope that women who read this book will become more cautious about concluding that their perspectives are not valid or that their desires are inferior. I would like for you to feel content with yourself, but at the same time I would like to encourage you to stretch yourself.

People who know me now in my forties cannot believe that I ever had low self-esteem, but I did. When I was a homemaker, I began to distrust my judgment about even simple things, such as which brand of green beans to buy! Repeating the same routine tasks over and over, I began to wonder if I could even do more difficult tasks. We were living in Wisconsin at the time and getting two babies dressed to go out seemed overwhelming in the cold winters, so I became more and more isolated.

After five years of taking care of babies, I decided to look into getting a graduate degree (since a bachelor's degree in psychology did not open up options for employment). I enrolled in my first graduate class after years of changing diapers, reading novels, and watching Perry Mason re-runs. I was very doubtful that my brain would be able to function and I was certain that everyone else in the class was from a much more mentally stimulating environment. But I made myself go to that first class. I took the notes I was supposed to take, read the texts I was supposed to read, and took the tests; still I was fearful that I would perform in a substandard manner, my brain having turned to baby powder. I got an "A!" And then I had the courage to take another class and another, until I had a master's degree. My confidence grew substantially. Starting a counseling center with my father was challenging, too. My confidence continued to grow. Next I started teaching, again taking on something hard, and was again rewarded. Now I can be on national television and *not* be all that nervous. This growth in self-esteem and self-confidence happened because I took on projects that were difficult for me. I stretched myself. The only way to feel confident about yourself is to stretch your-self. It doesn't have to be in a career; maybe it will be through something like mountain climbing, but find a way to stretch yourself.

In stretching yourself you will automatically create a life you enjoy. Only you can improve your situation, inside and outside, by using the solutions you learned in this book. Even if some-one else could do it for you, that would rob you of the wonder-ful chance for you to find out what is possible. I hope that you can feel how much I want you to have the power to make your life what you want it to be. I would hope that, from the mes-sages of this book, you now feel that it is as healthy and wonder-ful to do things for yourself as it is to do things for other people.

In stretching and taking care of myself, I have used every solution proposed in this book. I have examined my thinking and altered the questions I asked myself. I have changed my actions and patterns and communicated with others about the actions I wanted from them. I have used my unconscious to help me change my actions and feelings and explore my creative resources. I have used rituals to get over painful events from the past and to reconnect with myself. I *know* these solutions work.

As part of a ritual I would like you to create to keep yourself on track, I suggest selecting something visual—an object with meaning for you—and place it where you will see it often to remind you to use your solutions. It could be a picture, a poster,

on track, I suggest selecting something visual—an object with meaning for you—and place it where you will see it often to remind you to use your solutions. It could be a picture, a poster, a poem you write, a piece of jewelry you wear, or simply a phrase written on a three-by-five index card to remind you that you deserve to have a good life and that *you can create it*. I have a necklace, a crystal, that a woman friend gave to me as I was going through my divorce. I consider that necklace to be my reminder. When it is not around my neck, I have it hanging on my bed as a symbol of the power that I have to create the life I want. It has become a talisman of my power as a woman and of the love and support I feel from my women friends.

The support that I felt when I was going through difficult times is something I try to give to other women. Not only do I cherish my friendships, but I go out of my way to hire women for jobs: my accountant, my doctor, and my hairdresser are all women. Anytime I can help another woman, either by friendship or by directing business her way, I feel that I am adding to making the world a better place for all of us.

Even with help from other women and discovering the empowerment of stretching yourself, life will have disappointments for you, as it has for me. In those dark times I ask myself, *What are the solutions to learn from this experience and how can I take an active part in creating something better for myself?* I hope you will join me in choosing to create the life *you* want.

Bibliography

Bravo, Ellen, and Ellen Cassedy (1992). *The 9 to 5 Guide to Combating Sexual Harassment,* John Wiley & Sons, Inc., New York.

Campbell, Joseph (1968). *Hero with a Thousand Faces* (2nd ed.), Princeton University Press, Princeton, New Jersey.

Delaney, Gayle (1979). *Living Your Dreams,* Harper and Row, San Francisco.

Hudson, Pat (1993). *Making Friends with Your Unconscious Mind: The User's Guide,* Center Press, Omaha, Nebraska.

O'Hanlon, Bill, and Pat Hudson (1994). *Love Is a Verb: How to Stop Analyzing Your Relationship and Start Making it Great,* W. W. Norton & Company, New York.

Quinn, Jane Bryant (1991). *Making the Most of Your Money: Smart Ways to Create Wealth and Plan Your Finances in the '90s,* Simon & Schuster, New York.

Sommers, Christina Hoff (1994). *Who Stole Feminism: How Women Have Betrayed Women,* Simon & Schuster, New York.

Tannen, Deborah (1990). *You Just Don't Understand: Men and Women in Conversation,* Morrow, New York.

Tavris, Carol (1989). *Anger: The Misunderstood Emotion* (2nd ed.), Simon & Schuster, New York.

Tavris, Carol (1992). *The Mismeasure of Woman,* Simon & Schuster, New York.

Wolfe, Naomi (1992). *The Beauty Myth: How Images of Beauty Are Used Against Women,* Doubleday, New York.

Wolin, Stephen J., and Sybil Wolin (1993). *The Resilient Self: How Survivors of Troubled Families Rise above Adversity,* Random House, New York.

Index